TAKE TIME FOR
PARADISE

Exile and Change in Renaissance Literature

The University and the Public Interest

Play of Double Senses: Spenser's Faerie Queene

The Earthly Paradise and the Renaissance Epic

A Free and Ordered Space:
The Real World of the University

A Great and Glorious Game: Baseball Writings of
A. Bartlett Giamatti (edited by Kenneth S. Robson)

TAKE TIME FOR PARADISE

Americans and Their Games

A. Bartlett Giamatti

BLOOMSBURY

NEW YORK   BERLIN   LONDON   SYDNEY

Published by Bloomsbury USA, New York

All papers used by Bloomsbury USA are natural, recyclable
products made from wood grown in well-managed forests.
The manufacturing processes conform to the environmental
regulations of the country of origin.

LIBRARY OF CONGRESS CATALOGING-IN-PUBLICATION DATA

Giamatti, A. Bartlett.
Take time for paradise : Americans and their games / A. Bartlett
Giamatti; foreword by Jon Meacham.
    p.   cm.
Originally published: New York : Summit Books, c1989.
ISBN-13: 978-1-60819-224-3 (hardback)
ISBN-10: 1-60819-224-5 (hc)
  1. Sports—Social aspects—United States.   2. Leisure—
Social aspects—United States.   3. Baseball—Social
aspects—United States.   I. Title.
GV706.5.G53 2011
306.4'83—dc22
2010048207

First published in 1989 by Summit Books,
a division of Simon & Schuster

First Bloomsbury USA edition 2011

1 3 5 7 9 10 8 6 4 2

Typeset by Westchester Book Group

Printed in the U.S.A. by Quad/Graphics, Fairfield, Pennsylvania

To Abram and Kathryn Smith

CONTENTS

FOREWORD

Jon Meacham

As a Southerner, a Christian, and a baseball fan, I have long considered myself a man with a tragic vision of the world. To me there is a single inescapable fact of life on this side of Paradise: that the human enterprise to arrange things as we wish is ultimately futile. In hours of illness and danger, of decision and anxiety, we cry to the gods. Desperate and hungry and fearful, we plead with them to let the world unfold according to our hopes and affections.

Yet asking our gods—whoever they, or He, may be—to bend reality to our purposes has always been at best a chancy undertaking. No matter what we ask or offer, the innocent suffer, and the innocent die; some are rich, others poor; some lives seem charmed, others cursed. "The race is not to the swift, nor the battle to the strong," writes the cold-eyed author of the Book of Ecclesiastes, "neither yet bread to the wise, nor riches to men of understanding, neither favor to men of skill; but time and chance happeneth to them all." From the Hebrew Bible to *The Iliad* to the mythical American Camelot, a theme runs steadily through the human story. It was succinctly stated by our King Arthur, John F. Kennedy, who appreciated the ironies and tragedies of history. "Life," he once observed, "is unfair."

We are left, then, with the work of redemption—of seeking order, however fleeting, in the chaos, and love amid what the Book of Common Prayer calls the "changes and chances of this mortal life." Such is the function of familial and friendly *caritas*, of religion, of poetry, and of philosophy: the imposition of meaning and stability in a world in which all life, at least so far as we can know for certain, ends at the grave.

In the marvelous meditation of the following pages, the late A. Bartlett Giamatti—Renaissance scholar, president of Yale University, commissioner of Major League Baseball—turns to the deepest issues of human life and how the games Americans play at once restate the questions and point us toward some kinds of answers. Tracing the ideas of play, sport, city, religion, ritual, will, and imagination from farthest antiquity through 1989, the year the book was first published, Giamatti takes the greatest of American games, baseball, seriously—some might say too seriously, dismissing a book like this as an overblown effort to assign cultural, philosophical, and sociological weight to what is sometimes minimized by that falsest of phrases: *just a game.*

To wave baseball off as "just a game" is like referring to the global events of 1939–1945 as "just a war." No one can experience Giamatti's argument for the centrality and the significance of leisure—a concept that includes baseball—and come away without renewed or, for first-time readers, fresh respect for a mind and a heart capable of placing a pastime he loved in the full flood of time, not to the side or as an afterthought or as a distraction.

For Giamatti knew the tragedy of the game, and of life, in his bones; as he remarked elsewhere, baseball will always break your heart. Yet he also understood that the game has the capacity to allow its participants and its spectators—its priests and its congregants, if you will—to transcend the tragic, at least for a time. He thus arrives at a vision of baseball as a metaphor for the hunger for home, for security and sanctity and shelter from the storms of a transitory life. Think about it: a batter begins there, takes his chances and sometimes ends up on base, working his way around to . . . well, in the best of all possible worlds, to *home.* The journey is perilous and the wayfarers fail more often than they succeed—which, when you stop to ponder things, is true of many of us.

The joy, however, is in the journey, in the quest for the place you love, and where you are loved. "So home is the goal—rarely glimpsed, almost never attained—of all the heroes descended from Odysseus," writes Giamatti. "All literary romance derives from the *Odyssey* and is about rejoining—rejoining a beloved, rejoining parent to child, rejoining a land to its rightful owner or rule. Romance is about putting things aright after some tragedy has put them asunder."

Putting things aright: a noble goal, but one that is finally beyond us. Giamatti's brilliance is that he sees how baseball is, in the end, a story—a "Romance Epic," in his formulation—and we tell ourselves stories to stave off the disorder, to make sense of the insensible.

And not only we as individuals, but we as a nation. "If baseball is a narrative, an epic of exile and return, a vast, communal poem about separation, loss, and the hope for reunion—if baseball is a Romance Epic—it is finally told by the audience," Giamatti writes. "It is the Romance Epic of homecoming America sings to itself." It is American because it approximates America at her best: a level playing field, a fresh start every day, a value on merit, not birth, and a premium on practice, not publicity, for what matters on the field is what you do, not who you are; the plays you make, not the pay you take home.

This book was first published in 1989, in another time, another country, another world. Like the game itself, though, there is something eternal about its language, about its insights, about its truths. To read it again is to be pulled home; to read it for the first time is to hear the voice of a Homeric philosopher of a great game, an exemplar of intellectual engagement with the life of the nation that includes but is not limited to the Republic of Letters. Tragedy, romance, epic—it is all here, in this book as well as this life, and with this new edition comes a new season for Giamatti, and for all of us.

JON MEACHAM is the author of *Franklin and Winston: An Intimate Portrait of an Epic Friendship* and *American Lion: Andrew Jackson in the White House*, which was awarded the 2009 Pulitzer Prize. He is an unapologetic fan of the New York Yankees and of the Chattanooga Lookouts of the Southern League.

ACKNOWLEDGMENTS

My scholarly debts are acknowledged in the text and in the Bibliographical Note at the end. Here let me thank, again, Mildred Marmur for her guidance and assistance, and Mary Lou Risley for her indispensable efforts in preparation of the manuscript. James Silberman and Dominick Anfuso have been sensitive and scrupulous in their editing and support, and I am deeply grateful. My friend Fay Vincent cast his literate eye over the whole, and made it better. Bill Murray, baseball man, took the measure of Chapter 3. The errors that remain are all my own.

My thanks also to the faculty and students of the Law School of the University of Michigan. The School gave me the opportunity to deliver the 1989 Cook Lectures on American Institutions in which I first explored the material which appears in this book in a somewhat different form.

Last, I thank Marcus B. Giamatti for sharing with me his insights into two worlds he knows so well from the inside, those of the athlete and the actor.

—A. Bartlett Giamatti

PREFACE

It has long been my conviction that we can learn far more about the conditions, and values, of a society by contemplating how it chooses to play, to use its free time, to take its leisure, than by examining how it goes about its work. I am hardly the first to think so, and I trust I will not be the last. However unoriginal my conviction, it forms the basic assumption for this essay on Americans and their games.

Briefly stated, my argument is that sports are a subset of leisure and that properly to understand the allure and enduring appeal sports have for us as Americans, one must first understand the nature of leisure as that concept has developed since the Greeks, especially Aristotle. In order to place sports in that context, I found it necessary first to quarrel with some portion of the excellent work of Allen

Guttman, whom I regard as our most distinguished contemporary thinker on the nature and role of sport in society. I have adopted his basic view of sport as a rule-bound *autotelic*—that is, self-contained—activity and I assume as valid his scheme: *play* (spontaneous); *games* (organized play); noncompetitive games and *contests* (competitive games); intellectual contests and *sports* (physical contests).

I disagree with his basic assumption, variously expressed, that sport since the rise of the modern world, that is, after the Industrial Revolution, nearly 175 years ago, is profoundly different from sport previously. Sport has passed, Guttman would argue, from being a matter of ritual to being a matter (merely) of record.

Rather than argue that sports records exist as a form of immortality (and meaning) in a world that no longer believes in God, I argue that sports are in today's world what they were in yesterday's very different one—a shared moment of leisure. Sports represent a shared vision of how we continue, as individual, team, or community, to experience a happiness or absence of care so intense, so rare, and so fleeting that we associate their experience with experience otherwise described as religious or we say the sports experience must be the tattered remnant of an experience which was once described, when first felt, as religious. My argument is that in sports some version of immortality is being sought whether by way of ritual or of record, and that under the rubric of leisure, sport—either watched or played—has availed itself fully of whatever prestige or privilege accrues to shared activities that have no purpose except fully to be themselves. Throughout, I assert that the communal aspect of the experience is crucial.

Each of us sees our country and its institutions differently, yet we share them and share as well a generous vision, or a vision generous in its outlines, of them. Here is presented simply one man's view of our games and our country, that is, one view of some of our shared modes of seeing. Sport is an instrument for vision, and it ever seeks to make the common—what we all see, if we look—uncommon. Not forever, not impossibly perfect, but uncommon enough to remain a bright spot in the memory, thus creating a reservoir of transformation to which we can return when we are free to do so.

1

SELF-KNOWLEDGE

*If every day were holiday, to sport would be
as tedious as to work.*

HENRY IV, PART I, I.ii.205

WITH THAT GIFT for compression he would never lose, Shakespeare's Prince Hal teases us with some interesting truths, without fully meaning to do so. If "sport," which for him meant what "play" or "recreation" means for us, is opposed to "work," work is allied with tedium. And here we begin to glimpse the premises that will underlie this essay.

Work, as Hal implies, is tedious. It is tedious because it is done out of necessity, in order to survive. Work is partner to duty, and brother to obligation. Work is the burden we assume, not the one we choose. We may think, as humankind, that we choose our work, but very few of us since the dawn of life have had the choice *not* to work. Prince Hal's sport, our leisure, may be the alternative to work but only because work is the prior alternative to death.

Work is daylight existence. Without it, there is nothingness—no food, no shelter, no clothing, no family or community or civil state. "Work, for the night cometh," said Thomas Carlyle in *Sartor Resartus*, echoing Jesus in Matthew. Work, and keep the daylight of your life alive. Everyone recognizes the face of work. Occupations may vary and that variety may be interesting or instructive to observe, but the face of work is unchanging. It is the face you turn to the sun every day, or to its surrogate, the clock, so as to mark the passage of one's mortality and thereby also affirm that one is vital still.

Is work productive, "meaningful," fruitful, or, as so many hope, "fun"? Perhaps—though rarely always, and often never. It is, however, gainful, of the necessities and of those luxuries construed for whatever reason as necessary, and it is gainful of that necessity, that we be active, not inert. But whatever virtue we make of this necessity, work in this life is at its heart a negotiation with death, a bargain made daily in a thousand different ways until the strength to make that daily deal wanes, or the culture presses past one. Then not-work, retirement, only at its best leisure, ensues.

Then, when every day is holiday, that is, free from work, necessity cedes the day to choice. Then, the daily bargaining is with the self and not on behalf of staving off the end of existence. That is when, in our modern world where so many derive their only status from work, so many die. They find retirement to be idleness, not freedom; they find privacy to be—as the literary historian Michael O'Loughlin suggests it can be[1]—privation, not the pursuit of choice. They find that when they are not working, existence is as tedious as work, but that now it is an inactive tedium, a state of inertia—a form of death which can easily and painfully collapse from similitude into identity. These "retirees," in fact, die because they cannot bargain with themselves. There are no inner options. There was only, for them, the alternatives to be, through work, or not to be. There was never in their retirement what that other Shakespearean prince, Hamlet, learned so young and so late—to "let be": the option to choose, actively, among forms of life rather than simply between being or not.

Of course, most "retirements," most pursuits of holiday, do not result in people dying, or even patiently waiting for death by imitating it. Leisure, Prince Hal's "sport," is precisely choice, the use of free time. It is not passive, or merely private; it is not idle or inert. Leisure, engaged in either as participant or as spectator (and there have always been both, each existing for the other in a mysterious bond of energy, resentment, and awe), is that form of non-work activity felt to be chosen, not imposed.

Leisure, therefore, is so important, as a concept, as an index to a culture's condition, because it is a form of freedom and is about making free choices. As Prince Hal knows already, it is not only the opposite of work—not-work—but because he implicitly links "sport" and "holiday," he knows that leisure has some links to the sacred. "Holiday," when "sport" occurs, is, after all, a "holy day," a religious festival. Not all leisure is linked with specific festivals, but all leisure participates in a festive sensibility, or in the creation of such a sensibility. This is a state of inner being which is, or is like, the freedom from care and obligation and travail that is like a "religious" experience. Or it is an experience like what religion promises. If work is a daily negotiation with death, leisure is the occasional transcendence of death. If the former is the strenuous avoidance of inertia, the latter is the active engagement of a moment of immortality.

The seventeenth-century poet Henry Vaughan assures us he saw

> *. . . Eternity the other night*
> *Like a great ring of pure and endless light,*
> *All calm, as it was bright.*

What Vaughan describes is like a moment of leisure because it is, in Christian terms, a moment of contemplation. It is an instant of insight which is the result of freedom fulfilled, a state of coherence achieved with no coercion. Contemplation is the result not of work but of an activity freely assumed whose goal is to so perfect the self that for a moment we see what lies beyond the self— not as in an abyss, dark as night, but as in a radiance, bright as life.

Is it to argue fairly, however, about the religious-like condition of leisure by citing a religious poet at his mystical best as if that fragment were proof of the sacred tendencies of leisure? If there is a religious quality to our leisure—or even our games—does not that quality show itself in the intensity with which people follow sports, professional or amateur, rather than in the nature of the event either as rule-bound play or as a ritual occurrence?[2] Is it not true that transcendent values arise in relation to fishing or golf or the Washington Redskins because people invest those activities or groups with the values? Certainly it is true that if your knee is killing you, and your career— defined as either your athletic scholarship or your Olympic berth or your time in the pro League—depends on getting out there, and performing, then that is work, not play; that is your negotiation with inertia, and the only ceremony or festival is in the eye, heart, emotion, *rooting*, of the beholder.

If there is a truly religious quality to sport, then, it lies first in the intensity of devotion brought by the true believer, or fan. And it consists second, and much more so, in the widely shared, binding nature—the creedlike quality—of American sport. And building on that religious-like dimension, one could, if one chose, go to the view that sports in all their obsessive, overemphasized, wor-shipped forms are an opiate to the masses, a drug to keep people docile or at least diverted from real problems. In-deed, as we will see, some have argued that the rise of sport coincides with the rise of post-industrial society, that as people became alienated from work—which is perhaps nobler than I allowed—they were moved by the same capi-talist forces into mass amusements, now cheapened and inauthentic, and finally only another product of industrial economies.

To conclude this line of argument, sports, after the spinning jenny and cotton gin, after Blake's *Songs of Inno-cence and Experience*, after Dickens's *Hard Times*, are not re-ligious in any serious way. They are industrial. They are mass entertainment. As Allen Guttman so well argues, because of secularism, equality, bureaucratization, speciali-zation, rationalization, quantification, and the obsession with records, there is no link to the sacred or transcen-dent.[3] The record has replaced the ritual. "When we no longer distinguish the Sacred from the Profane or even the good from the bad, we content ourselves with minute discriminations between the batting average of the .308 hitter and the .307 hitter. Once the Gods have vanished from Mount Olympus or from Dante's Paradise, we can no longer run to appease them or to save our souls," says Guttman, "but we can set a record. It is a uniquely modern form of immortality."[4]

In the main, I agree with the argument that sports can be viewed as a kind of popular or debased religion, in the sense that the most intense feelings are brought to bear or in the sense that sports may mirror whatever avowedly "sacred" concerns Americans do share. Whether sport is solely a people's religion or only the amusement of an industrial society (commercialized sport as mass entertainment), either assertion essentially rests upon a premise I do not share: that all sport is radically different after the rise of post-Enlightenment industrialism—that before the rise of industrialism (the modern world), games and contests and sports in all cultures retained a mythic or religious or ritualized role or relationship to some transcendent source of values, and that since then these same pursuits are merely nonutilitarian forms of activity. Games and sports, by this premise, are merely rites that have lost their sacred signification and reflect all the characteristics of an industrial society, including the absence of sacred meaning or memory.

By this view, sport, even for its most serious interpreters, is trivialized at the very moment it is most weightily analyzed because sport is seen merely as the remains of a vanished world. At its worst, sport is the pointless, if widely enjoyed, detritus of an industrial society—a kind of non-toxic pollutant, junk food for the spirit, without nourishment, without history, without serious purpose. At its best, sport is the remnant of an Edenic world, now gone, mere maypole dance without the maypole—fun, redolent of nostalgia, and, probably because of the physical exertion required, good for your heart or maybe your character, but no longer meaningful for serious folk, except, of course, as occasions to moralize. All this because the maypole now carries telephone lines.

Here we are at the crux of the matter. I believe that much of the foregoing about a people's religion, and, indeed, about the commercialization of sport, must be retained in any view of modern Americans and their games. But I also believe that the perspective on our sports, or the West's, which argues that sport's sacred connections are clearly lost, and that therefore records have replaced ritual, misperceives leisure, the condition of being in which sport, or athletics, plays merely a part.

It was, after all, in Leisure that this chapter began, with Prince Hal. What we have seen, I hope, is that there is no quarrel with the notion that in freely chosen leisure activities, games or others, more can be told of a culture's (or individual's) condition than in tedious work, for to pursue leisure is to use freedom, our most precious possession—

whether defined as a day off, as free time, or as the political condition aspired to by a people. But beneath this assumption, beneath Hal's opposition of sport and work, is the alliance Hal made between sport and holiday, and that conjunction is not Christian, much as in the West we tend to receive, and reject, it in Christian terms. It is ancient— which means Greek, for us. And unless we place whatever we think about America and her games in the context of Greek (and subsequent) thinking on leisure—rather than in the context of comparative anthropology on sacred games in all cultures or sociopolitical theories of the decline of culture-wide Christian values, neither of which is the appropriate context, one far too wide, one far too narrow—we will never grapple with what Prince Hal, or his creator, summed up in one line and our culture enacts in its way every day.

Leisure is a vast subject, and the scholarship on it very rich. Our best guide is the brilliant study by Michael O'Loughlin already alluded to. As O'Loughlin points out, the Greek word for *leisure* is *scholē*, the same Greek word that gives us *school*. As he says, "What they had in mind as 'free time' survives in what we still appropriately call the 'liberal arts.'"[5] He is referring to the classical concept of leisure as being at one with classical and, hence, modern theories of education, not so much in terms of subject matter as in purpose. Just as what Roman, and Renaissance, culture called the *studia humanitatis* or *artes liberalis* were to be pursued because in their pursuit the muscle that is the mind was disciplined and toughened and thereby made more free, to pursue new knowledge, and just as that freedom in the mind became a freedom for the mind, which freedom is the precondition to and guardian of political or social freedom (this theory of education as clear to Jefferson as to Aristotle, and I hope, for our sakes, as clear to us as to them), so was the pursuit of these studies undertaken in, and meant to perpetuate, a condition of leisure. That is, a condition of mind and spirit fulfilling itself through the exercise of choices whose goal was to maintain the freedom to exercise the mind. So pure play and schooling that pursues knowledge for its own sake, and leisure or free time, are all at last connected conceptually.

They are *all* autotelic activities—that is, their goal is the full exercise of themselves, for their own sake, because in them a condition is achieved that is active, not idle; entertaining, not simply useful; perfecting of our humanity, not merely exploitative of it. In the circularity of self-fulfillment—in pure play, liberal study, and "free time"—a condition of freedom of spirit is actively induced and consumed, as a nourishment. That condition simulates what is promised, or provided, by religious experience—a state of contemplation, vigorous and expansive, of the highest force conceivable. The result is to be careless, or carefree. It is to be happy.

But to return to O'Loughlin's expansion on *scholē*, the

Greek word for *leisure*: "Significantly, it is business that the Greeks defined negatively, calling it 'un-leisure' (*a-scholia*), just as the Romans opposed *otium* to *negotium*. The emphasis is more than any etymological curiosity. 'We do without leisure . . . ,' writes Aristotle in a famous formulation of priorities, 'only to give ourselves leisure.' "[6]

O'Loughlin is citing Artistotle's *Nichomachean Ethics*[7] where in discussing happiness as consisting of acting in accordance with the virtue, and finding happiness to be in contemplation, the highest, active virtue, Aristotle says, "Also happiness is thought to involve leisure, for we do business in order that we may have leisure and carry on war in order that we may have peace." Indeed, Aristotle has in the *Politics* returned repeatedly to this formulation, and theme, saying at one point that it is "the first principle of all things"[8]—that, as he says elsewhere, ". . . life as a whole is divided into business and leisure, and war and peace, and our actions are aimed, some of them at things necessary and useful, others at things noble . . . war must be for the sake of peace, business for the sake of leisure, things necessary and useful for the purpose of things noble."[9]

For me, Aristotle focuses the lens. The opposition is not between useful work and pointless (or non-utilitarian) sport, with sport in the modern world having lost its religious meaning and retaining as its only role to be a mirror of secular, modern life. The issue is not a dualistic opposition between work and play. It is a progression from one to the other, from what is necessary to what is desirable, from the utilitarian to the liberal, or free; from what, as Sebastian de Grazia suggests, dignifies (work) to that which perfects (leisure).[10]

O'Loughlin adds another dimension to the concept of leisure: ". . . the condition of leisure which today we think of as a private privilege would seem to originate in, and be first sanctioned by, a supra-personal awareness, an allegiance to the classical *polis*, for example, or to the Christian Kingdom of God."[11] In short, whether classical or Christian, leisure as an ideal was a state of unforced harmony with others; it was, ideally, to live fully amidst activity, which activity has the characteristic of free time.

Throughout Western culture, the highest status has been conferred on such communal, leisure activities. If there is a break in the last 150 years, it is not that we have lost touch with, or faith in, the gods of Olympus or of Dante's Paradise. Rather it is that we have lost any primary contact with, or sense for, the setting that those various versions of God reflected: the dominant ideas and their forms of expression that create (and transmit) our Western culture. Before American games are American, they are Western, even those invented, like basketball, in America, because they are played and perceived within a context of values, assumptions, and desires that have been developing much longer than the recent history of some particular society's interpretation, or manipulation, of a given game.

For instance: A man goes to a college football game on Saturday afternoon because, it is assumed by his neighbors, in part he is gripped by the point spread—that is, he is interested in the outcome of the game for gambling purposes as much as he is interested in the rule-bound autotelic activity, the game. Because he is using the game to gamble with friends, and because the culture seems to encourage gambling by printing the point spread and broadcasting it, and because he finds some like-minded co-workers at his law firm or brokerage house or investment bank or insurance company, thus manufacturing the corporate culture's self-image as one made up of risk-takers, those who would be "players," people for whom doing the deal is in the long run as much fun as getting the fee, because of all these factors, one could examine the role football plays for individuals or for corporate culture and muse on and extend the implications of that constellation—corporate America, patriotic symbols, football the territorial game—and then expatiate on military-industrial postwar America, the rise of professional football in the late forties and fifties, and feelings of inadequacy at the weakening of American global hegemony being compensated for by fanatical devotion to football's command, control, and strategic dimensions. And so forth.

And if one notes that this kind of ball game has no transcendent meaning any more, no connection to sun worship or phases of agriculture but only to a society that is suffering from what the historian Paul Kennedy has called "overstretched imperialism," one could carry on and quite forget that our football fan's neighbors are wrong. Our football fan is going to watch a game he loves, because he has played it. It reminds him of his best hopes, when he was young and supple. There is a ritual to how he dresses and to where he parks or eats or sits or what he drinks, small, homemade rituals but in their way important to his pleasure, which is after all the purpose of the whole afternoon—as pleasure might be the goal of his life as well.

His rituals are part of larger rituals: of sharing a fine, clean, snapping autumn afternoon, of hearing some favorite music, as evocative in its own powerful way as football is for him but now just another pleasure in the whole pageant of pleasures, a pageant that also includes the crowd, its clothing, its colors, its rivalries, its common joy, the comradeship of competition. Very soon the crowd is no crowd at all but a community, a small town of people sharing neither work nor pain nor deprivation nor anger but the common experience of being released to enjoy the moment, even those moments of intense disappointment or defeat, moments made better, after all, precisely because our fan is part of a large family of those similarly affected, part of a city of grievers. When people win together, the joy is more intense than when any of us wins alone, because part of any true pleasure is sharing that pleasure, just as part of the alleviation of pain is sharing the burden of pain. Finally, we should note, our fan has entered an arena or stadium which may look more like its ancient precursor than anything else in the modern world looks like its architectural ancestors. The gods are brought back when the people gather.

All of this our fan experiences, and we have made no real reference to the game, to the occasion for all this pleasure, including the emotion of losing—which brings pleasure only in the limited but real sense that bonds to others are forged again and bitterness cannot break them. The game on the field enacts as well repetitive or ritualistic patterns, those inherent in playing (although all players of any game are also spectators with special vision), rituals of play far more highly honed and charged with personal significance than even the rituals of watching. The point is, sport is ceremony wherever you find it. It mimics the ritual quality of religious observances even when sport is no longer, if it ever was, connected to a formal religious act of worship. In that mimesis, however, an experience akin to the religious is engaged in over and over.

For the sport's participant, it is an experience of the constant dialectic of restraint and release, the repeated interplay of energy and order, of improvisation and obligation, of strategy and tactic, all neatness denied and ambiguity affirmed by the incredible power of the random, by accident or luck, by vagaries of weather, by mental lapses or physical failure, by flaw in field or equipment, by laws of physics that operate on round or oblong objects in their own way, by error in all its lurking multiplicity. It is not news that there is the snake of error in our lives; the news occurs when, for a moment, we can kill it. News occurs in winning, and knowing what that feels like.

The spectator apprehends all this, at one remove. His energy, and frustration, and hunger for order are those of the *voyeur* who would be a *voyant*, the spy from the edges of the clearing who longs for the experience of the seer, the vision of triumph at the center of the clearing. The spectator invests his surrogate out there with all his care-free hopes, his aspirations for freedom, his yearning for transmutation of business into leisure, war into peace, effort into grace. To take the acts of physical toil—lifting, throwing, bending, jumping, pushing, grasping, stretching, running, hoisting, the constantly repeated acts that for millennia have meant work—and to bound them in time or by rules or boundaries in a green enclosure surrounded by an amphitheater or at least a gallery (thus combining garden and city, a place removed from care but in this real world) is to replicate the arena of humankind's highest aspiration. That aspiration is to be taken out of the self. It is to be for a moment in touch, because common pleasure is so intense, with a joy that cannot be described because language has limits and can finally only say what is *not*, but falters before an experience which so completely *is*.

When we watch a contest or sport, and internalize the deep fact that this is an activity that has no ultimate consequence, no later outcome, no real effect beyond itself, we invest it with tremendous significance because in this world of history and work and endless, tangled consequence, to have no "real" consequence or sequel is such a rare event. And when in the midst of that free time activity (as we understand the meaning of leisure) a person on the field or fairway, rink, floor, or track, performs an act that surpasses—despite his or her evident mortality, his or her humanness—whatever we have seen or heard of or could conceive of doing ourselves, then we have witnessed, full-fledged, fulfilled, what we anticipated and what all the repetition in the game strove for, a moment when we are all free of all constraint of all kinds, when pure energy and pure order create an instant of complete coherence. In that instant, pulled to our feet, we are pulled out of ourselves. We feel what we saw, become what we perceived.

It is a moment when something not modern but ancient, primitive—primordial—takes over. It is a sensation not merely of winning, for the lesson of life is that you cannot win, no matter how hard you work, but of fully playing: as the gods must play, as whoever is not us—call it the Deity or History or whatever is Untrammeled—must play, complete, coherent, freely fulfilling the anticipated fullness of freedom. It is a sensation of playing because fully free, as whatever superior forces you cannot control at all must play, as the wind must play with the sun and flowers again on a soft, spring day.

In that moment of vision, of sensation compounded of sight and insight, everyone—participant and spectator—is centered. No one is eccentric. All work is dissolved into free time. The essential ceremonial quality of sport, made of anticipation, repetition, and fulfillment, has worked to force the noblest expression leisure can provide—the state of contemplation that is, as Aristotle wrote, "the activity of the intellect that constitutes complete human happiness."[12] It does not last a whole life span, as Aristotle says it should last; it lasts mere moments. But it is no less authentic for that. The memory of that moment is deep enough to send us all out again and again, to reenact the ceremony, made of all the minor ceremonies to which spectator and player devote themselves, in the hopes that the moment will be summoned again and made again palpable.

The gods have fled, I know. My sense is the gods have always been essentially absent. I do not believe human beings have played games or sports from the beginning merely to summon or to please or to appease the gods. If anthropologists and historians believe that, it is because they believe whatever they have been able to recover about

what humankind told the gods humankind was doing.
I believe we have played games, and watched games, to
imitate the gods, to become godlike in our worship of
each other and, through those moments of transmutation,
to know for an instant what the gods know. Whether
celebrated by Pindar or Roger Angell, sport is, however,
ultimately subversive of religion because while it mimics
religion's ritual and induces its fanaticism and sensation,
sport cares not at all for religion's moral strictures or political power or endless promises. Sport cares not for religion's
consequences. And though I cannot prove it, I do not believe
sport ever has cared. It cares for itself, in that uniquely
free, ceremonial, and subversive way I have attempted to
describe.

If playing sport is akin to another human activity, it is
akin to making art. When scholars, like the estimable
Guttman, tell me, for instance, "To the degree that Greek
athletic festivals were religious ritual and artistic expression, they had a purpose beyond themselves and ceased to
be sports in our strictest definition of the terms [that is,
rule-bound autotelic activities]. The closer the contests
came to the status of art, the further they departed from
that of sport,"[13] I beg to dissent. Because athletic events
contained to some degree religious ritual as well as artistic
expression does not mean that all the rituals were for identical purposes or even sought an identical goal. One could
argue, in fact, that coincidence of occurrence meant there

were thought to be a variety of routes to the same goal, or even to analogous goals—that athletes, like artists, proffered their own versions of enhanced life, as priests do. Some commentators seem to think that because an activity has no goal beyond itself, it therefore has no purpose. The purpose of autotelic activity, whether called play or study or leisure or artistic activity, is to fulfill itself without regard to consequence, and in that fulfillment to achieve a state of being, as I have suggested, that is like what religion often describes, but which is not the sole possession or province of religion, and which does not need ever to be described in religious terms. When in another context O'Loughlin refers to the "artistic transformation of life which might be called the central myth of leisure,"[14] he is on the mark for describing sport.

At the core of a view of leisure, and hence of my view of sport, is my essential difference from all the commentators for whom sport is the precipitate of a once far richer solution that was called sacred play or religious worship. I believe sport in Western culture has functioned occasionally as a part of religion but much more expansively and powerfully as part of our artistic or imaginative impulse. Sport is autotelic activity, if you will, transformative of *negotium* to *otium*, tedium to freedom (in Aristotle's terms, war to peace), *because* it is a medium for self-transformation. Differently but nevertheless in concert, participant and spectator seek that *agon*, that competition with self to make the self over, to refashion or refigure or re-form the self into a perfect self, over and over again, in sport. In that contest, for the players, lies the essential competitive urge, which is the urge to self-expression, self-expression that masters and controls self and others, that overwhelms whatever is disparate or random within one and in one's environment, including other players and spectators, and that forges or forces a coherence—a victory of one's own. A "win" is the actual realization of what is centrally an imaginative surge. To compete with others successfully, one first wins out over oneself, and so controls and fulfills one's interior, if one is truly gifted, such that one's surroundings can only succumb.

The spectator, seeing something he had only imagined, or, more astonishingly, had not yet or would never have imagined possible, because the precise random moments had never before come together in this form to challenge the players, is privy to the realized act of imagination and assents, is mastered, and in that instant, bettered. "Winning" for player or spectator is not simply outscoring; it is a way of talking about betterment, about making oneself, one's fellows, one's city, one's adherents, more noble because of a temporary engagement of a higher human plane of existence. Records, and they have existed since the Greeks,[15] are simply one form of memorial (statues, inscriptions, poems, trophies of all kinds, and oral tradition or word-of-mouth being some others) for a moment otherwise lost. They are necessary, because the most poignant fact about sport has always been the transitory nature of achievement. Thus we have the urge to memorialize but, even more, to seek to re-create the instant of immortality by playing or watching again and again.

Recreation is re-creation, the making again according to some standard in the mind, vision in the head, in the hopes of making what one imagines, palpable. The painter or sculptor, poet, architect, or composer, whether he worships a deity or not (and there is nothing to stop him from saying he does even if he does not, or from accepting commissions from the deity's earthly representatives regardless of personal belief), is basically driven to express what begins as a gnawing hunger and becomes a rage to perfection. Or, if "perfection" is too troublesome a word, a rage to get it right, to make things fit as they never have before, to show a sight or make a sound that is as completely coherent, as fully a law unto itself, as close to completely what glistens within, as possible. On the spectrum of artists, it is those at the other end—the performers, the actors, dancers, musicians, singers—who most clearly resemble athletes, in that they all interpret a preexistent creation, though in their re-creation there is much of the kind of primary hunger for control and expression that went into making the initial artifact, whether play or symphony, ballet, opera, song, or game. As performers, they all form or re-form through the conventions of the artifact, so as to transform themselves and others.

Athletes and actors—let actors stand for the set of performing artists—share much. They share the need to make gesture as fluid and economical as possible, to make out of a welter of choices the single, precisely right one. They share the need for impeccable and split-second timing. They share the need for thousands of hours of practice in order to train the body to become the perfect, instinctive instrument to express. Both athlete and actor, out of that congeries of emotion, choice, strategy, knowledge of the terrain, mood of spectators, condition of others in the ensemble, secret awareness of injury or weakness, and as nearly an absolute *concentration* as possible so that all externalities are integrated, all distraction absorbed to the self, must be able to change the self so successfully that it changes us.

When either athlete or actor can bring all these skills to bear and focus them, then he or she will achieve that state of complete intensity and complete relaxation—complete coherence or integrity between what the performer wants to do and what the performer has to do. Then, the performer is free; for then, all that has been learned, by thousands of hours of practice and discipline and by repetition of pattern, becomes natural. Then intellect is upgraded to the level of an instinct. The body follows commands that precede thinking.

When athlete and artist achieve such self-knowledge that they transform the self so that we are re-created, it is finally an exercise in power. The individual's power to dominate, on stage or field—and they are versions of the same place and are only by analogy altars—invests the whole arena around the locus of performance with his or her power. We draw from the performer's energy, just as we scrutinize the performer's vulnerabilities, and we criticize as if we were equals (we are not) what is displayed. This is why all performers dislike or resent the audience as much as they need and enjoy it. Power flows in a mysterious circuit from performer to spectator (I assume a "live" performance) and back, and while cheers or applause are the hoped-for outcome of performing, silence or gasps are the most desired, for then the moment has occurred—then domination is complete, and as the performer triumphs, a unity rare and inspiring results. When power is ineffective or dispersed, then fragmentation or division or simply solitariness occurs in the arena, the communal experience sinks back into crowd behavior, and ordinary life—what we came to be free of—shows itself in the place of leisure, and is all the more bitter because, for Heaven's sake, we came to be better.

All play aspires to the condition of paradise. By that I mean that through play in all its forms, including through professional sports in late twentieth-century America, we hope to achieve a state that our larger Greco-Roman,

Judeo-Christian culture has always known was lost. Where it exists, we do not know, although we always have envisioned it as a garden, sometimes on a mountaintop, often on an island, but always as removed, an enclosed, green place. *Paradise* derives from the Avestan word *paridaēza*, for enclosure, meaning the enclosure or park of the King. In the Old Persian, it meant a noble or special enclosure, as it did in ancient Hebrew, as well as, after Greek and Latin cognates were applied to the Garden in Genesis 2:8, meaning the garden in Eden. Paradise is an ancient dream, only Christian after it was first Assyrian, Persian, Hebrew, Greek, and Roman. It is a dream of ourselves as better than we are, back to what we were.[16]

Aristotle taught the West to ally schooling with this redeemed sensibility, to make *scholē* the root of school. But even Aristotle could not keep the verdant imagery out of the compound he so successfully made between school and play, the mind in freedom striving to surpass the mind's limits. We preserve the imagery still in our word *kindergarten*, the child's garden at beginning of schooling and time of first play, and perpetuate it, as George Williams notes in *Paradise and Wilderness in Christian Thought*, in our college and university courtyards and quadrangles, all the enclosures, like the Cloisters, we cherish to sequester still the free play of the intellect.

But it is the condition of freedom that paradise signals,

and that play or sport—however hedged in by the world—wishes to mirror, however fleetingly. And while I have insisted on saving sport from being trivialized by those who would charge it with being empty of religious content, and therefore crass, by arguing that a theory of leisure should govern our view of the role and purpose of sport, I nevertheless wish to close this chapter by invoking paradise as a general condition, though not as a specific doctrine. The condition is to live in a physical and mental world of choice where every choice is free of error. After Milton's Adam has told Eve that their only stricture is not to touch the fruit of the tree of the Knowledge of Good and Evil, he says,

> . . . let us not think hard
> One easy prohibition, who enjoy
> Free leave so large to all things else, and choice
> Unlimited of manifold delights.
>
> (Paradise Lost, IV. 432–435)

Save for the prohibition, those lines capture the essence of Aristotelian leisure better than any I know, the ideal to which our play aspires:

> Free leave so large to all things . . . and choice
> Unlimited of manifold delights.

But in fact, the serpent was already there, and our sports do not simulate, therefore, a constant state. Rather, between days of work, sports or games only repeat and repeat our effort to go back, back to a freedom we cannot recall, save as a moment of play in some garden now lost.

2

COMMUNITY

B Y CLAIMING SPORT as a form of Aristotelian leisure, not as a remnant of primitive religion, I have urged a view of sport as a means, like art, of self-transformation through self-knowledge. And, fully possessed of the courage of my aberrations, I was willing to assert that sport was the daily re-creation of the impulse of pure play, a reiteration of the hunger for paradise—for a freedom untrammeled. While acknowledging this view as the description of an ideal, I am also willing to insist that this ideal is powerful and persuasive. Whatever the realities, we scorn or ignore at our peril, at the risk of the loss of awareness and pleasure, those qualities of sport that are autotelic and ceremonial. To shun or denigrate sport because it more often fails to reengage its highest promise—for player or spectator—is to undervalue the power of that promise. To say sport rarely if ever achieves the garden ideal ought in no way presume to deny the ideal's existence.

This chapter will explore sport as it lives in the world, to the east of Eden, not on a mountaintop but in the valley. Assuming sport is autotelic and ceremonial, this chapter will focus on sport as it is conventional and commercial; assuming that play (and games) aspires to the condition of paradise, we must remember that (contests and) sports also flourish in, and are in every sense most deeply allied with, the City. Where *scholē* seeks a state of green and growing thoughts, a garden of the mind, sports as we know them—physical contests pitting individuals or teams against each other—are city-bound, that is, connected to cities or to the creation of a city. This means sports are conventional and commercial. To explore how and why, we must first consider broadly the nature of a city.

When musing on cities over time and in our time, from the first (whenever it was) to today, we must always remember that cities are artifacts. Forests, jungles, deserts, plains, oceans—the organic environment is born and dies and is reborn endlessly, beautifully, and completely without moral constraint or ethical control. But cities—despite the metaphors that we apply to them drawn from biology or nature ("The city dies when industry flees"; "The neighborhoods are the vital cells of the urban organism"), despite the sentimental or anthropomorphic devices we use to describe cities—are artificial. Nature has never made a city, and what Nature makes that may seem like a city—an anthill, for instance—only *seems* like one. It is not a city. Only human beings have ever made cities, and if cities were patterned on nature, they were patterned—some claim—on the seemingly fixed stars and constellations, that crowd of settlers so vast in number and enduring in brilliance. But to adopt a natural pattern is no more to let Nature make a real city than to adopt a simile or metaphor from Nature is to define a city.

Human beings made and make cities, and only human beings kill cities, or let them die. And human beings do both—make cities and unmake them—by the same means: by acts of choice. We enjoy deluding ourselves in this as in other things. We enjoy believing that there are forces out there completely determining our fate, natural forces—or forces so strong and overwhelming as to be like natural forces—that send cities through organic or biological phases of birth, growth, and decay. We avoid the knowledge that cities are at best works of art, and at worst ungainly artifacts—but never flowers or even weeds—and that we, not some mysterious force or cosmic biological system, control the creation and life of a city.

We control the creation and life of a city by the choices and agreements we make—the basic choice being, for instance, not to live alone, the basic agreement being to live together. When people choose to settle, like the stars, not wander like the moon, they create cities as sites and symbols of their choice to stop and of their agreement not to sepa-rate. Now stasis and proximity, not movement and dis-tance, define human relationships. Mutual defense, control of a river or harbor, shelter from natural forces—all these and other reasons may lead people to aggregate, but once congregated, they then live differently and become dif-ferent.

A city is not an extended family. That is a tribe or clan. A city is a collection of disparate families who agree to a fiction: They agree to live *as if* they were as close in blood or ties of kinship as in fact they are in physical proximity. Choosing life in an artifact, people agree to live in a state of similitude. A city is a place where ties of proximity, activity, and self-interest assume the role of family ties. It is a considerable pact, a city. If a family is an expression of continuity through biology, a city is an expression of continuity through will and imagination—through men-tal choices making artifice, not through physical repro-duction.

This act of will and imagination, this city, expresses a set of common and continuing needs. Those needs are usually expressed as commercial. Cities, we are told, are essentially mediums for commerce—trading, buying and selling, fi-nancing. They are centers of negotiation, not simply in all the varieties of commerce, but also of lawmaking and rule-giving—of legislation in all its variety. Cities are cen-ters of negotiation of interests, of competing ideas, of us together against separateness, of me against aloneness—of all that was noted in Chapter 1 as entailed at first by work, the work of connecting and assaying, of affiliating and discriminating that markets and legislatures, commerce and courts, traders and advocates carry on.

But for all that negotiation describes a city's life, its defining characteristic over time is neither strictly commercial nor legal. The defining characteristic of a city over time is political. Indeed, the word *political* contains at its root the Greek *polis*, or *city*. Politics is the art of making choices and finding agreements in public—or the art of making public choices and agreements. Politics is the ultimate act of negotiation in a city, but is only reflective of the constant activity of the city, as individual, daily choices and agreements and decisions, all flowing from the central choice not to live alone but among others, swirl around and make up rambunctious, noisy, restless, demanding, hectic, city life.

Over millennia, this refinement of negotiation—of balancing private need and public obligation, personal desire and public duty, and keen interests of the one and of the many into a common, shared set of agreements—becomes a civilization. That is the public version of what binds us. That state is achieved because city dwellers as individuals or as families or as groups have smoothed the edges of private desire so as to fit, or at least work in, with all the other city dwellers, without undue abrasion, without sharp edges forever nicking and wounding, each refining an individual capacity for those thousands of daily, instantaneous negotiations that keep crowded city life from being a constant brawl or ceaseless shoving match. When a city dweller has achieved that truly heightened sensitivity to others that allows easy access, for self and others, through the clogged thoroughfares of urban existence, we call that smoothness *urbane*. We admire the capacity to proceed, neither impeded nor impeding. If our origins or sentiments are rural in orientation, we may not trust that *urbanity*, for it may seem too smooth, too slick, but we cannot help but recognize in it a political gift in the deepest sense.

To be of the *urbs*, to be urbane, is to be political and to be civilized. Throughout the several millennia of our Western culture, to be urbane has been a term of high praise precisely because cities are such difficult environments to make work. There are so many competing and unique needs to be accommodated, so many deals to be struck simply to get from here to there. So much work just getting to work. Many give up, and, like the rurally minded Horace or Pope, or most clearly Dickens's truly suburban Wemmick in *Great Expectations*, they go to the suburbs, that under-city that is neither urban nor rural, that non-city which is the place of surcease, not of choosing—where energy, to the extent it is desired, is imported but not created; where all decisions are basically private and existence is nonpolitical; where in choosing to give up the stress of endless

42

choosing, there is only one choice: to live *not as if* in a family but rather to live *as if* alone, and to do so near similar (that is, like-minded, like-colored, like-employed) families. To be suburban is to live in retirement while still actually at work; it is to have the illusion of *otium* while caught up in *negotium*. And when more than some—when many—opt for the suburb, the city begins to die. When those who can make the choice leave, by that choice a city falters because it retains only those who have no choice but to stay. Where cities are absorptive and inclusive, suburbs are not. Their impermeability or exclusivity is precisely their allure.

But over time, most cities are chosen again, and are refashioned. For all the allure of speciously stress-free suburbs, for all the grinding of city life, cities endure. And when all those diverse energies are harnessed, and those choices, private and public, cohere, and all the bargains made in a million ways every day hold up, then a city flourishes and is the most stimulating center for life, and the most precious artifact, a culture can create. Think of great cities large and small (size, as with any work of art, does not necessarily determine value) and, in addition to nodes of government, commerce, law, hospitals, libraries, and newspapers will come to mind, as will restaurants and theaters and houses of worship and museums and opera houses and galleries and universities. And so will stadia and arenas and parks. In short, one finds not simply commerce but culture, not simply work but leisure, not only *negotium* but *otium*, not simply that which ennobles but also that which perfects us. Such has forever been the ultimate purpose of a city, to mirror our higher state, not simply to shelter us from wind and rain. As with leisure, so with the city: It is the setting to make us not the best that Nature can make us, but to manifest the best we, humankind, adding Art to Nature, can make us.

We encounter sports in cities, or find sports striving to make a city-like—communal and civil—environment wherever they are pursued because sports and cities share a common characteristic: They are deeply conventional. A convention is an agreement, an agreed-upon fiction, a done deal. A convention is whatever is made—a stage from elevated boards, a treaty from pieces of paper, a set of social manners, a system of law—by common consent. It is the social agreement we all make to act *as if*. It is a design of our making rather than by the seeming randomness of Nature's. A convention is a social pattern we have chosen to prefer over whatever the raw world simply proffers. It is a sign of the operation of the mind, drawing the assent of a sufficient number of other minds so that the agreement will be widely operative. A convention is not a custom; a custom is a habit in which a sufficient number acquiesce. A custom can appear as a convention, but it is really a lesser act, the result of passive acceptance rather than of the imposition of design. It is the difference between learning to live by the annual flooding of the river or by a calendar. In this view, all games are conventions, all cities are conventions—ultimately all culture is a convention, particularly if we remember that *culture* means tilling the soil in patterns and with purpose, making, as Thoreau said, the earth say beans instead of grass, that is, putting design and shape into a common environment, beginning in the mind whence all design flows.

The conventional quality of contests or sports, as I have construed them, is obvious. It lies in the fact that games are rule bound. Rules—complete and completely arbitrary— are what set these activities off from work, and make them doorways to leisure. Or, in the terms of this essay, make them artifacts, that is, entirely created by human will and imagination, social agreements for organizing energy that make no sense except in their own terms.

Sports are conventional, and are self-contained systems of convention. Indeed, our sports are so refined and de-signed—so rule bound and internally complete, with lore and custom as well as their own rules or law—that they can have the character of *cults*, those closed-off, self-contained cultures that demand one's total being, one's to-tal assent.

The cultic dimension of sports—with the attendant fanaticism of some fans, and the complete absorption into the temple such that nothing else obtrudes or matters to many athletes—is dangerous. A convention, like a sport, negotiates between the tedium of life and work and a world of special privileges, of release, seemingly of total freedom. It mediates between what we have and what we want and provides a version of the latter in the midst of the former. But whatever mediates retains elements of the initial polarity. It is a third thing that partakes of the first two things and does not remove itself from their world entirely, else no one would agree that it mediates. When we veer into the special world of a sport in order to live there, rather than to visit, sport as mediator dissolves and cult displaces convention. In the cult, drugs or alcohol can take on a special significance, as a way for adepts—the initiates—to affirm their membership in this closed culture and to signal their specialness. Drugs or alcohol, shortcuts to specialness, can also be mistaken as a way to find advantage, an edge, meaningful only in that world.

Sports become cults when the sport convention is too strong for some. For some—particularly young professional athletes with no other strong culture or collegiate athletes without any role in the culture of college life except to be mercenaries (that is, those for whom there is so little else in the way of intellectual or familial or social ties outside sports)—it is easy to succumb to the cultic lure of the special world of sports. This is especially true if pressures exerted by expectations in the media and from coaches or parents are never countered by other expectations or demands. Many of the abuses, including the abuse

of drugs or alcohol or steroids, among some college athletes or some professional athletes, stem from the complete athletization of life, the displacement of all general
social rules by the rules of the game's culture. Totally
absorbed, some feel invulnerable, invincible, completely
exempt from conventional expectations and from the demands of other conventions, and completely protected
from sanction.

It is not the fault of athletes if they are given, from the
earliest age that they show a special gift, the belief that
they inhabit a special world or that they must—for someone else's satisfaction—be entirely immersed in a special
world. Parents, coaches, teachers, and later, if the young
athlete is truly gifted, professional teams' management as
well as lawyers, agents, business managers, and perhaps by
now also a spouse, not to mention journalists and groupies
and hangers-on, and those with a deal, or something to
sell, or an invitation, or an advertisement, or a charity, not
to speak of fans (of all ages and conditions, bound in ado-
ration or, at least, oversized admiration)—all may seemingly conspire, while never meaning to, to do harm by
constantly assuring the young person that a gift for sport,
particularly a lucrative and popular one, is the most important (indeed, the only important) feature of his or her
life or of his or her role in their lives. The "conspiracy" is
rarely intentional. It simply occurs from the concentration
of separate hungers focusing on the young athlete. Because

an athlete is raised to imitate, to follow the leader, to be a team player, the athlete obeys.

If the game or sport is very strong, and those the young athlete loves or who say they love the athlete want the athlete to live their fantasies to the exclusion of all else, life in the cult may be the young person's fate. When it is, the inevitable result, particularly among some former professional athletes well into their thirties (although I have seen it among college athletes and, in a few cases, with unusually gifted high school athletes whose "careers" stopped at about nineteen), is that there is no place in the general culture for them when they no longer fit in the cult. They have prepared no skill or trade, have eschewed all other interests, have made no plan or expressed any desire for a plan, because no one told them or they refused to believe that there comes an end to running, an end to the cheers, an end to the life lived on the cuff, an end to the endless pleasuring of themselves. They never grow up in any real sense, because they were meant always to be young and strong and special, somewhere in late adolescence in fact, and that expectation was one they shared. They are profoundly innocent. Such people are as if newborn when it is over, accustomed to packing a suitcase but not to carrying it very far, unaccustomed to making hotel or airplane reservations, to keeping a checking account, to waiting in line, to being interviewed for a job, unaccustomed to few if any of the hundreds of daily activities that require one to negotiate for oneself. I say this not to blame anyone. Blame or guilt is not the issue. The issue is to warn us against giving over our young as hostages to any powerful social convention, even one as seemingly innocent or pleasurable as sports.

Cult occurs when the convention *of* a sport is too strong, when common consent overrides an individual's internal culture or a family's common sense. (If the convention *of* the sport is weak, it fades away, like cricket in America in the mid- to late nineteenth century.) Chaos occurs when the convention *in* a sport is too weak. Here we turn from looking at the convention of sport to the convention within a sport, to the way all sports are composed of innumerable conventions, just as the ceremony of a game is compounded of many smaller ceremonies.

The formal conventions within a sport are, to say the least, numerous. There are the rules governing play and players—League or Conference or Association or Olympic or NCAA rules as well as the rules laid down for professionals in collective bargaining. There are the team rules, from Pee Wee Hockey to Pop Warner to Little League on up, governing practice, deportment on and off field, and often play—either formally or informally (as in the team's "game plan" or signals or signs). For professionals and students receiving "grants-in-aid," there are contracts of various kinds. There are the rules governing access by the media—sports are part of the entertainment business, and even when athletes are amateurs, most journalists covering them are not. There are the university or college or school rules governing the place or role of athletes or athletics within the total institution. There are the ownership rules in professional sports franchises, those business or behavioral rules laid down by the top management. There are finally the fans' rules—not simply rules governing the area or venue, mostly designed to protect fans from each other and players from fans, but rules also designed to keep the environment surrounding the game from intruding on the primary reason all those rules exist, which is the playing of the contest that day. I might add that sports officials, who uphold the rules of play, live under most of these rules and some special ones of their own, too.[17]

All these rules are conventions, meant to separate the sports world from the quotidian world, meant to organize energy into a contest, meant to be an internal compromise, balancing restraint and release so as to ensure competition. By imposing identical conditions and norms upon play, the essential assumption of all the rules is that skill or merit, not chance, will win out.

These rules express expectations, the basic one being that everyone understands the completely artificial nature of the game or contest or sport and understands the injunctions, therefore, to abide by all these *sui generis* regulations, else the whole enterprise has no meaning. After all, if one is not going to accept that basic convention, none of the others makes sense, just as if one rejects the convention that art is an expression of a kind of reality, whether "representational" or not, then none of the conventions beneath the initial suspension of disbelief has any reference. One might as well live in Nature, red in tooth and claw.

When the conventions within a sport are weak, Nature in fact does pour in, just as when a dike is weak, water will press through. Conventions, after all, are meant as stays against chaos. For instance, if the enforcement of the rules of play in a sport is lax or ineffective, by intention or not, then the contained energy will get loose, and violence will occur, rather than whatever physical contact the sport releases in order to restrain. When this happens, the violence on the ice or floor or field is not different from what one might encounter on the street outside the arena. Of course, if the sponsors of the sport at the professional level and the spectators want that new element of violence, it soon becomes conventional. Fighting becomes stylized, an agreed-upon interlude during play. The sport changes. College players—then eventually high school players—imitate the professionals. A whole game is now changed as the new convention for fighting works its way into the sport. The distance between the game and a daily reality the game is meant to transmute lessens.

A more serious, because premeditated, act in sports is

cheating. Violence, after all, grows organically from the energy expended in playing a physical contest; even the most professional player, who is, after all, deeply competitive, can lose restraint and explode. But violence over time is uncontrollable only when officialdom does not rigorously enforce the rules. Cheating, however, has no organic basis in a game. It is a premeditated act that strikes at a basic convention: that if everyone plays by identical conditions and rules and with identical equipment in a contest designed to declare a winner, skill or merit—sheer ability—will win the day. Of course, one knows other factors may enter into a victory, but they are random occurrences of Nature or human frailty and cannot be accounted for in a convention. The basic convention for any game is the assumption of a level field, that all begin as equals, aboveboard. Without that convention, there is no contest.

Cheating—a covert act to acquire a covert advantage—strikes at the heart of this basic convention of openness and equality and the agreement that they are essential. If the other internal agreements of the sport or its rule-makers do not defend the sport, if cheating is not dealt with swiftly and severely, the game will have no integrity—that is, no coherence of conventions, no internal authenticity. Spectators will very rapidly lose interest if they think they cannot trust the game to deliver the fairness it promises.

The highly moralized (because rule-bound) world of any sport is very fragile in the face of the amoral quest for betterment, the hunger to win at any cost, even at the cost of destroying the game, the game being the only context where winning in this way has any meaning whatsoever. Cheating is a constant temptation to those who have honed so keenly the competitive edge, who strive for betterment through sport, and it has been ever since Odysseus cheated in the Funeral Games near the end of the *Iliad*. When the rules designed to sustain the convention that lawful skill (or skill lawfully applied) can win the day, that the game is a meritocracy, are weak or not enforced, then the quest for a covert edge will always threaten to shatter the whole enterprise.

When those running a sport do not believe their own conventions, then the essential convention of a sport as a meritocracy in every sense will be undermined. When laxity on that scale occurs, then cheating on a large scale metastasizes. Then the social cheating of racism can occur. For instance, when baseball desegregated itself in 1947 on the field, the first American institution ever to do so voluntarily (before an executive order desegregated the U.S. Army, and before the Supreme Court, the public schools, and Congress passed the Civil Rights Act of 1964), baseball changed America. Baseball changed how blacks and whites felt about themselves and about each other. Late, late as it was, the arrival in the Majors of Jack Roosevelt Robinson was an extraordinary moment in American history. For the first time, a black American was on America's most privileged version of a level field. He was there as an equal because of his skill, as those whites who preceded him had been and those blacks and whites who succeeded him would be. Merit will win, it was promised by baseball.

Baseball thereby made a tremendous promise—to play the game of America by the rules of the Constitution and the American Dream—and when it failed to deliver completely, it cheated itself and the country by not entirely fulfilling the very promise it had voluntarily made. Its central convention, of equality being the ground for merit competing, was, for men of color after their playing days, largely a myth, not a solid convention. Baseball in all its parts was not as willing to afford to former players of color those opportunities to be trained and to compete for positions in the ranks of those who manage (in every sense) as it had for a long time been willing to provide opportunities for white former players. It still must provide the opportunity to let merit compete fully. At least now the game at the Major League level recognizes that, like America, the sport has a racist past, and knows it must once again strive to lead the country in expunging whatever vestiges of racism remain. Baseball at the Major League level must continue to strive to make that central meritocratic convention strong, coherent, and authentic, and it will.

My central point is that games in their various versions are social agreements to live by, instrumentalities to make our common life pleasurable. When these social agreements are too "strong," then social injury results when our common life is, for some, displaced by cultic life; when these social agreements are "weak," because they are not agreements at all but fictions, social injury results because someone is deceived for someone else's advantage. When one says the sport is "healthy," a biological metaphor applied to this artifact just as it is applied to a city, then we really mean, as we do with a city, that all the conventions cohere and are abided by, at least to the extent that adverse social costs of any kind are at a minimum. When this condition is achieved in that work of art that is a city, people choose to live there; when it is achieved in that social artifact that is a sport, people choose to continue to watch it or, in sufficient numbers of the talented, continue to participate in it.

Sports and cities, sharing a deep conventionality, have always been allied. Not that there are no rural games; there are. And there are certainly conventions ruling, or making possible, rural life. But rural contests tend to be less rule bound (hunting and fishing—contests between man and nature—are recreations, not contests) and more allied to the daily rhythms of rural work; rural conventions are familial not simply in origin (most conventions are that), but in focus. In rural pastimes, as in rural life, custom plays a more prominent role. All of this is the result of a simple fact: Where large masses of people live, a deeper or broader or more refined, in the sense of nuanced, sense of conventionality and set of conventions are necessary to make life bearable and perhaps pleasurable—my view of the political essence of a city. And that same mass of human beings will create, and refine, the convention of sports to reflect their urban environment, their urban gift.

We see this influence reflected in the basic sports venue. From Greece and Rome to today, that venue is some version, grand or small, of the arena or amphitheater. It may be in a rural setting or in the middle of a city; it may be an old, bowl-type coliseum (a name in constant use, recalling its Roman archetype), or it may look like the popular concept of a spaceship—another version of urban design imitating supposed galactic patterns. But wherever it is and however it is shaped, the sports venue is urban in that it arranges in more or less orderly fashion, according to class or economic standing—that is, by price—a large mass of people. It is a small city—at once a market, a forum or a meeting place, a house of worship if you wish, a crowded neighborhood or seemingly massively extended family— often split in factions, the basic dualism of Us and Them, a dualism at the heart of all sports where two parties compete—in all kinds of ways a special, set-aside-in-the-midst-of-life indoor or outdoor little city.

The little city is special in various ways: If outdoors, it may be completely enclosed, or may not be, but in either case, the spectator is surrounded, if not completely in structure, certainly in crowd, and in expectation. The spectator and participant accept the convention, as one does in a theater, that the life about to be displayed is not real (as distinct from a house of worship, where the claim is that life is more real, the reality of our essence or ultimate end), but different, an enhanced life, not a final one, a life in costume. Uniforms may be *uniform* and thus useful in telling apart the sides, that is, in distinguishing the two parties to this mock dispute that is about to be settled, but uniforms are also costumes, important for identity, colorful, designed to enhance ease of performance—a life strenuously lived *as if.*

And to signal the artifice, the striving to achieve a state of living *as if,* is the conjunction of arena and field, of city and garden, the enclosure of the stadium delineating the people's paradise of the field. Indeed, baseball—the most strenuously nostalgic of all our sports, the most traditionally conscious of tradition, the most intent on enshrining its rural origins (which it knows were on June 19, 1846, on the Elysian Field, in Hoboken, New Jersey, when Alexander Cartwright's team played another team by the first set of rules for grown-ups, but which loves its Cooperstown, its rural *mythos* of upstate New York, rather than its astonishing reemergence of Elysium in classicizing New Jersey)— baseball still calls these playing fields, wherever they are, "parks." Football, with soccer, calls them "fields"; hockey calls them rinks, and replicates a frozen pond indoors.

Basketball—the only truly urban invention (but played not only in cities but wonderfully throughout largely rural areas, like Indiana and China)—calls them floors, but dresses for this indoor, winter game in the most outdoorsy, summery way. (It is the only great game most American men have *always* been willing to play in shorts.)

Tennis and golf are different. They have the most genteel, not to say aristocratic and ancient, origins, and have longest maintained their aura of privilege. A tennis court is not an urban phenomenon; it is a "courtly" one. It can today be found in cities, and the great tourneys take place in cities—I know of no great, culminating sporting event that is not coupled with a city (I exempt the Kentucky Derby and the Indianapolis 500 from all this; they are great events but not sports in my terms because while human beings compete, they do not provide the energy)—and in enclosures of great refinement, surrounded by serried banks of spectators. Tennis courts, however, are everywhere as other venues are not—who has a football field at home? Pools and tennis courts are signs of social status when found, as they are in many cases, in private homes.

So, occasionally, are putting greens, though almost never entire golf courses. A golf course is the least urban venue possible, deriving from and signaling the most privileged origins. Golf retains the hallmarks of its genteel aspirations in being still one of only two major games played competitively—and nothing is more competitive than golf—where spectators do not make noise during play. Golf is the only sport where one can have a servant do the work[18] while one does the play, and where there is a gallery to watch it all (for that is the name by which this collectivity of spectators is called, a name that has urban connotations and that recalls something of the quality of an extended group of retainers, the household watching the Lord of the Manor at play). The Lord can play the game alone and find it fulfilling; only of bowling, the most ancient game or contest, and curiously—for here priority signals no privilege—associated with the other end of the social ladder, can one say that as well. (One can say it of basketball, but I do not believe it is fulfilling to play alone. It is simply possible.) Bowling is the other sport where knowledgeable spectators do not make noise during play.

But even an urban tennis court and certainly a fairway, with its green goal, remind us of the garden world, the condition of leisure where all play aspires to paradise. Thus, whether in a real city or not, when we enter that simulacrum of a city, the arena or stadium or ballpark, and we have successfully, usually in a crowd, negotiated the thoroughfares of this special, set-aside city, past the portals, guarded by those who check our fitness and take the special token of admission, past the sellers of food, the vendors of programs, who make their markets and cry their news, and after we ascend the ramp or go through the tunnel and enter the inner core of the little city, we often are struck, at least I am, by the suddenness and fullness of the vision there presented: a green expanse, complete and coherent, shimmering, carefully tended, a garden—even indoors where wood or ice stands in for grass (or the far greener artificial equivalent of grass), the effect is similar.

And whether there is, indoors or out, a wall or barrier separating spectator from player, whether bunting or music or mascots or marchers or leaping creatures in costume or advertising images gambol there, eventually the eye finds a device, hanging or looming, to tell the time and give the details and figure forth the score. This device knits up all the conventions, those the spectators (who make the city) bring, and those the players (who animate the garden) live with. It is a device whose refined capacities to reflect the action would be meaningless anywhere else in the wider or surrounding city. The scoreboard is the symbol of this garden-city's specialness. It tracks the negotiations that matter; it makes official whenever *negotium* achieves *otium*.

Why will the largest number of people, wherever they congregate, create and consume leisure in ways that reflect their deeply rooted aspirations for sports (garden) and their own skills (city)? Because, it is worth reminding ourselves, that is the way we have fun. Fun is, after all, the immediate purpose of the enterprise. It is necessary, however, if no fun, to remind ourselves that our word *fun* is probably derived from the obsolete verb *fun*, meaning *hoax* in the seventeenth century, itself probably a dialect variant of the obsolete *fun, to make a fool of*. After the word meant *hoax* (seventeenth century), it came to mean *sport* or *diversion* in the eighteenth century. When you are having fun, the English language believes, you are fooling yourself. "Sport" is based, here at least, on a practical joke, which is to say that sport is serious, but it is a trick, an illusion—not real. That is the deepest way sport is conventional—it is a conscious agreement to enjoy, a pleasurable self-delusion.[19] If sport aspires to contemplation, let us remember it begins in a con.

The other immediate purpose of the enterprise of games in America, and here we are firmly in the modern world, urban or not, is commerce. Indeed, in America, we should properly speak of the commercial nature of leisure, for if leisure was *scholē* for Aristotle, it was a $50 billion business for America in 1987. So as we began our first chapter by placing sport within leisure, we can end the second by looking for sport in the commerce of leisure.

In November 1988 *Sports inc.*, a weekly devoted to the business of sports, presented its second annual Gross National Sports Product. The author of the report, Richard Sandomir, worked with the Wharton Econometric Forecasting Associates Group, and drew from manufacturing, trade, sporting, and other sources and from the data and methodology of the U.S. Department of Commerce. The

Category	1987 Revenue Generated (in millions)
Leisure and participant sports	$16,480.0
Sporting goods	16,278.4
Advertising	3,623.6
Spectator sports receipts	3,300.0
Net take from legal gambling	2,842.0
Concessions, souvenirs, and novelties	2,100.0
TV and radio rights fees	1,209.2
Corporate sponsorships	1,012.0
Magazine circulation revenues	685.6
Royalties from licensed sports properties	584.0
Athlete endorsements	520.0
Golf course construction	400.0
Trading cards and accessories	350.0
Stadium and arena construction	250.0
Sports book purchases	241.0
Pro team sports insurance	180.0
U.S. Olympic Committee and national governing bodies budgets	98.2
Youth team fees	95.3
Halls of fame	5.4
TOTAL	$50,209.7

Gross National Sports Product, construed as "the sum of the output and services generated by the sports industry," in 1987 totaled $50.2 billion.[20] That total was up 6.1 percent from the 1986 GNSP, and meant that the sports industry was America's twenty-third-largest industry, bigger "than the auto and security and commodity sectors of the United States' $4.52-trillion national economy, . . . not much smaller than the paper and printing and legal industries, as measured by the Gross National Product."

This view of the sports industry includes much, though hardly all, of what we would define as recreational or physical leisure. Therefore, assuming the following categories include more activities than I have denoted within this essay by the word *sports* but fewer than we know Aristotle meant by *scholē*, what are the elements of the American sports industry?

This is a very big business, or set of allied businesses, and almost surely will grow in 1988 to something around $52 billion. Astonishingly, only 6.6 percent of this GNSP is composed of revenues from live spectator sports even though, as the report notes, those sports consume "most public interest." And this means that, despite the extraordinarily high visibility and drawing power of some sports at the professional level and at what America still insists on calling, in certain instances, the "amateur" or "collegiate" level, the culture, in terms of its pocketbook, is going elsewhere in its "free time," at least in its recreational free time. Where the pocketbook leads, the heart will follow.

In fact, it is obvious where leisure is going. It is going private. What hitherto in American, or indeed Western, culture had always been initially personal, and therefore, I have argued, potentially communal and civic, is now simply private, to be neither shared nor explained. In the last two decades, there has been one striking image of the privatization of recreation or leisure time—the solitary jogger. I know one can jog or run with others, and I am sure there is a cable channel, a newsletter, three hotlines, and a foundation in Santa Barbara all devoted to propagating the virtues and tax advantages of communal jogging. Common sense tells me, however, that if you jog, you jog alone. We have all seen the recent version of that figure, a creature neither male nor female, costumed head to toe, sweatband to special shoes, in muted sweat clothes scrupulously shapeless, earplugs plugged, the music—like the clothes—"designer made" to the individual taste, the American Androgyne chasing good health, which is itself the most elusive dream of immortality. Solo jogging is certainly a leisure activity and it aspires to the paradise within, happier far, but it is not civic or communal. No city comes of it.

The jogger tailors leisure to him- or herself, outdoors. The other great private practitioners of leisure are indoors. They—I mean those in their late teens or younger—are the beneficiaries of one of the great revolutions in technology, comparable to the introduction of movable type in the fifteenth century. As with that innovation, so with this one: The marriage of the integrated circuit and the screen (indeed, all the technology of how imagery is transmitted and displayed) is a revolution in how seeing is seen, in how thinking is thought about.

New video technology changes the meaning of meaning. Where the transition from page to screen is incomplete for anyone born before 1950, because for such people even a simple television screen will always, at some deep recess, be a novelty, for the young the screen in any form is the most familiar piece of furniture in the mind because it is the medium that formed the mind. The stately television set (towing its dinghy, the VCR), the word processor, the Personal Computer, the video game—screen in all its manifestations including films and scoreboards—all have the same authenticity as the printed page, and, for many, more authenticity, more power.

And for the millions of children and young people for whom MTV is the norm for how one sees, theirs is a way of seeing very different from the older generation's. The older generation absorbed information at a far slower rate, less (or is it more?) atomistically, less passively, in black and white, in one dimension, as on a page; for the young, data can be absorbed at a far, far faster rate, but fresh new stimuli are needed to hold the attention. The young assume the pre-organization, the pre-selection, of what is to be known. If they can absorb quick cuts, they assume tight editing. And finally, they can take in, without being repulsed or disturbed, vast quantities of input that are not representational—not realistic-looking. These youngsters are, and will be, less conventionally minded, that is, less dependent for amusement, or even leisure, on agreed-upon signs and images to make a different reality, because they are more plastic, more absorptive, far more tolerant of shapes and bargains that never appeared before in art or nature. They may also be less aware of—or may need less of—the sustaining power of traditional convention. They may be less interested in the socially cohesive force of already agreed-upon signs and widespread social agree-ments, and in the cohesive value of that social force. They will have new (visual) conventions of their own.

The options for leisure, for filling and fulfilling free time, will grow. Video technology has only begun to go everywhere on earth, live—and we have merely scratched outer space. I marvel at it. We cannot foresee the things to be seen. The inclination to privatize leisure will be fed by the capacity to do so. Spectator sports could gradually, over two generations, a half century, become either antiquarian pageants, like the Sienese horse race called *Il Palio*, or stu-dio events, played indoors in temperature-controlled en-vironments, with the equivalent of laugh tracks, or raucous remnants of a faded world, amusements for those who cannot get out of cities or afford the gear to see the Soviet Army play the U.S. Air Force in "spaceball," a likely spin-off of volley-ball, on a platform off Mars. Spectator sports could well become such things unless those responsible for the public's pleasure in public places realize that there is nothing inherently magical about their games. What is magical is the experience sought by player or spectator through games or sports.

If those who enjoy the prestige, visibility, and money attendant upon managing spectator sports do not maintain that 7 percent of the GNSP, by convincing the jogger to come occasionally and sit down with others, and by convincing those indoors in front of a screen to come occasionally out to the park, then Sport will not change its autotelic, ceremonial, conventional, and commercial nature, but spectator sports will change, some to fade, others to become stylized or stripped versions of themselves, others to go with curling or hurling into very small and specific communities.

So, let me close this chapter by raising a banner for the spectator, the average fan whose presence is crucial to the public presentation of sports: Public places require constant care—they require cleanliness, reasonable order, coherence, and accessibility; they require attention to parking lots, rest rooms, alcohol management, and reasonable audiovideo policies on giant scoreboards; they require awareness that the older, traditional fans, for whom the contest is a ceremony, and the less conventionally minded, younger fans, for whom the contest is an occasion for their own separate pleasure, must both be accommodated so that the energy, the fervent zeal, the rousing excitement, and the happy camaraderie of competition we so value when we come together can continue to flourish for masses of us in the artificial but real confines of that special world, set aside but urban, the stadium holding paradise, the public place for public pleasure.

3

BASEBALL AS NARRATIVE

SOME CONTESTS DERIVE directly from work—where else do careb throwing or rodeo events come from?—some from war, like archery or fencing or, perhaps, the javelin throw, some from primitive forms of combat, like boxing or wrestling. But regardless whence a contest or sport derives, its appeal will be on very personal, not deeply historical, grounds. We will watch or play games or sports that reflect how we think of ourselves or that promote how we wish to be perceived.

Our pleasure, however, whose origins are far more difficult to discover than are the historical roots of any sport or game, is radically tangled up with our childhood. Much of what we love later in a sport is what it recalls to us about ourselves at our earliest. And those memories, now smoothed and bending away from us in the interior of ourselves, are not simply of childhood or of a childhood game. They are memories of our best hopes. They are memories of a time when all that would be better was before us, as a hope, and the hope was fastened to a game. One hoped not so much to be the best who ever played as simply to stay in the game and ride it wherever it would go, culling its rhythms and realizing its promises. That is, I think, what it means to remember one's best hopes, and to remember them in a game, and revive them whenever one sees the game played, long after playing is over.

I was led to these thoughts by thinking on my own love of baseball, and the origins of that emotion. And then I was led to this last chapter by the opening lines of a poem by Marianne Moore called "Baseball and Writing":

> *Fanaticism? No. Writing is exciting*
> *and baseball is like writing.*
> > *You can never tell with either*
> > > *how it will go*
> > > *or what you will do.*

Serendipity is the essence of both games, the writing one and baseball. But is not baseball more than *like* writing? Is not baseball a form of writing? Is that not why so many writers love baseball? To answer this question, we will turn third and test our initial assumptions.

If it is instructive as well as pleasurable to think about

how America produces and consumes its leisure, then I believe thinking about baseball will tell us about ourselves as a people. Such thoughts will test two propositions. The first is that baseball, in all its dimensions, best mirrors the *condition of freedom* for Americans that Americans ever guard and aspire to. The second proposition is that because baseball simulates and stimulates the condition of freedom, Americans identify the game with the country. Even those indifferent to baseball, or country, or those who scorn them, at some level know them. The rest of us love them.

To know baseball is to continue to aspire to the condition of freedom, individually and as a people, for baseball is grounded in America in a way unique to our games. Baseball is part of America's plot, part of America's mysterious, underlying design—the plot in which we all conspire and collude, the plot of the story of our national life. Our national plot is to be free enough to consent to an order that will enhance and compound—as it constrains— our freedom. That is our grounding, our national story, the tale America tells the world. Indeed, it is the story we tell ourselves. I believe the story in its outline and many of its episodes. By repeating again the outline of the American Story, and placing baseball within it, we engage the principle of narrative. We posit an old story, sufficiently ordered by the imagination so that the principle of design or purpose may emerge.

What are the narrative principles of baseball, its over-plot? At its most abstract, baseball believes in ordering its energies, its content, around threes and fours. It believes that symmetry surrounds meaning, but even more, forces meaning. Symmetry, a version of equality, forces and sharpens competition. Symmetrical demands in a symmetrical setting encourage both passion and precision.

We see this quality best when we consider baseball's plot not as story line, but plot as soil, the concrete grounding. The field, the literal plot of the game, consists of a square whose four sides are ninety feet long; this square is tipped so that a "diamond" is enchased in the grass. Not quite in the middle of the square, sixty feet, six inches from home plate, is a circle, with a radius of nine feet, at whose center (we are on the pitcher's mound) is a "rectangular slab of whitened rubber, 24 inches by six inches."★ So far, all the dimensions are multiples of three.

This last rectangle is the central shape in the geometry of the field, set within but not parallel to the larger square of the "diamond." The circle of the mound faces a larger circle around home plate, whose radius is thirteen feet, containing three squares, two of which, for batters, are six feet by four feet. The third is marked only on three sides, is forty-three inches wide, and is of undetermined length.

★The distance from the pitcher's rubber to the front edge of home plate is fifty-nine feet, one inch. The rubber itself is one inch behind the center of the pitcher's mound.

The square of the diamond is contained in a larger arc or partial circle, whose radius, measured from the center of the rectangular pitcher's slab, is ninety-five feet. The perimeter of this (partial) circle denotes the grass line running from foul line to foul line at the outer infield or innermost outfield. The bases are rectangular, fifteen inches square. The foul lines extend from the tip of home plate along the sides of the ninety-foot square to first and third. These perpendicular lines theoretically extend to infinity. In fact, since June 1, 1958, they are obliged to extend at least 325 feet until their path is interrupted by a fence (just as there must be a minimum of four hundred feet in the line from home plate to the center-field fence).

How to characterize the structural principles grounding this game? Squares containing circles containing rectangles; precision in counterpoint with passion; order compressing energy. The potentially universal square, whose two sides are foul (actually fair) lines, partially contains the circle, whose radius is at least four hundred feet and whose perimeter is the circle of the fence from foul line to foul line, which contains the circle of the outer infield grass, which contains the square of the diamond, containing the circle of the pitcher's mound and squares of the three bases. The circle of the mound contains the rectangle of the pitcher's slab and faces the circle of the home-plate area, which contains the rectangles of the batter's boxes and the area for umpire and catcher. At the center of this circle, and existing in eternal tension with the pitcher's rectangle—seemingly the center of such power, of so many dimensions—is the source of the macro dimensions, the point of reference for all the medium and the larger geometric shapes, the only shape on the field that does not figure the eternal and universal outlines and meanings of square and circle. We are at home plate, the center of all the universes, the *omphalos*, the navel of the world. It, too, plays around fours and threes, but altered, a shape unique. The *Official Baseball Rules*:

> Home base shall be marked by a five-sided slab of whitened rubber. It shall be a 17-inch square with two of the corners removed so that one edge is 17 inches long, two adjacent sides are 8½ inches and the remaining two sides are 12 inches and set at an angle to make a point. It shall be set in the ground with the point at the intersection of the lines extending from home base to first base and to third base; with the 17-inch edge facing the pitcher's plate, and the two 12-inch edges coinciding with the first and third base lines. (1.05)

This curious pentagram is central in every sense to the concentric circles and contending rectangles of the place. It is also deeply disruptive of their classic proportions and their exquisitely choreographed positions and appositions. Home plate mysteriously organizes the field as it energizes the odd patterns of squares tipped and circles incomplete. Home plate radiates a force no other spot on the field possesses, for its irregular precision, its character as an incomplete square but finished pentagram, starts the field, if you will, playing. It begins the dance of line and circle, the encounters of energy direct and oblique, of misdirection and confrontation, of boundary and freedom that is the game, before any player sets foot on the field. Home plate also has a peculiar significance for it is the goal of both teams, the single place that in territorially based games—games about conquering—must be symbolized by two goals or goal lines or nets or baskets. In baseball, everyone wants to arrive at the same place, which is where they start.

In baseball, even opponents gather at the same curious, unique place called home plate. Catcher and batter, siblings who may see the world separately but share the same sight lines, are backed up and yet ruled by the parent figure, the umpire, whose place is the only one not completely defined. This tense family clusters at home, facing the world together, each with separate responsibilities and tasks and perspectives, each with different obligations and instruments. Some are intent on flight, some on communication, some simply on the good order of it all—the "conduct of the game"—but they are still a family or family-like group in their proximity, their overall perspective, their chatter and squabbling, their common desire, differently expressed, to master the ferocity and duplicity of that spherical, irrational reality—the major league pitch.

But I anticipate. The geometry of the field that extends the threes and fours gives as well the deep patterns that order the narrative—three strikes, three bases, nine players, nine innings; four bases (including home) or four balls (the walk which is escape, the commencement of movement that might fulfill the quaternity of the diamond). Three and its multiples work in baseball to delimit, to constrain, to be the norm that, except for duration, cannot be surpassed. Only nine innings may be lawfully overgone—baseball having no clock and, indeed moving counterclockwise, so anxious is it to establish its own rhythms and patterns independent of clock time.★ But even that extension beyond nine exists because there must be a winner, an ending, that is definitive. How a game ends is itself interesting; the closure of any narrative always is. Baseball ends with the home team having the final say, the guests having opened the narrative.

The central triad of strikes and outs telescopes out into three by three, giving us a game with a definite beginning, middle, and end, a well-made play in three acts, of six scenes to an act, three to a side. Put another way, if three strikes were the lot of every batter on one side, then

---

★ Although see *Official Baseball Rules*, 8.03 and 8.04, setting time limits of pitchers.

twenty-seven batters would have to go up and go down on one side to fulfill a perfect game. But there is a greater perfection—that the maximum of twenty-seven, which is also a minimum, go up and go down for both sides. That ultimately perfect game could theoretically endure in time like the foul lines in space—indefinitely. Our meditation has found the One, but where is the game?

If extrapolation may drive baseball's organizing numerology and patterns to a sterile (and impossible) perfection, only repetition can bring satisfaction. The game on the field is repetitious—pitch after pitch, swing after swing, player after player, out succeeding out, half inning making whole inning, top to bottom to top, the patterns accumulating and making organizing principles, all around and across those precise shapes in and on the earth. Organized by the metric of the game, by the prosody of the play, is all the random, unpredictable, explosive energy of playing, crisscrossing the precise shapes in lines and curves, bounces and wild hops and parabolas and slashing arcs. There is a ferocity to a slide, a whispering, exploding sound to a fastball, a knife-edged danger to a ball smashed at a pitcher— there is a violence in the game at variance with its formal patterns, a hunger for speed at variance with its leisurely pace, a potential for irrational randomness at variance with its geometric shapes.

The game is all counterpoint. The precise lines and boundaries and rules, and all the scholastic precision baseball brings to bear on any question, on every play, only serve to constrain the sudden eruptions of energy, the strenuosity of the game, and thus to compound the meaning and joy of accomplishment. We recall that the patterns of rhyme and the rules for pivot and recapitulation in a sonnet compress the energy of language, and compound significance. But cannot the same be said of turning a double play, where the rhythm and force, pivot and repetition are the whole point? The point being that freedom is the fulfillment of the promise of an energetic, complex order?

If baseball is a Narrative, it is like others—a work of imagination whose deeper structures and patterns of repetition force a tale, oft-told, to fresh and hitherto-unforeseen meaning. But what is the nature of the tale oft-told that recommences with every pitch, with every game, with every season? That patiently accrues its tension and new meaning with every iteration? It is the story we have hinted at already, the story of going home after having left home, the story of how difficult it is to find the origins one so deeply needs to find. It is the literary mode called Romance.

While it may be fanciful to construe the cluster around the plate as a family, it is certainly not a fancy to call that place "home." That is the name of the odd-shaped pentagram. Home plate or home base. I do not know where it clearly acquired that name. I know that the earliest accounts of the game, or an early version of it, in children's books of games in the early nineteenth century, call the points around the field—often marked by posts—"bases." The game was called "base," though in his diary a soldier at Valley Forge with Washington called it "baste."[21] I know Jane Austen tells us at the beginning of *Northanger Abbey* that Catherine Morland played "base ball" as well as cricket, thus distinguishing them. But none of these early references clarifies whence came the name for "home." Why is home plate not called fourth base? As far as I can tell, it has ever been thus.

And why not? Meditate upon the name. *Home* is an English word virtually impossible to translate into other tongues. No translation catches the associations, the mixture of memory and longing, the sense of security and autonomy and accessibility, the aroma of inclusiveness, of freedom from wariness, that cling to the word *home* and are absent from *house* or even *my house*. *Home* is a concept, not a place; it is a state of mind where self-definition starts; it is origins—the mix of time and place and smell and weather wherein one first realizes one is an original, perhaps *like* others, especially those one loves, but discrete, distinct, not to be copied. Home is where one first learned to be separate and it remains in the mind as the place where reunion, if it ever were to occur, would happen.

So home drew Odysseus, who then set off again because it is not necessary to be in a specific place, in a house or town, to be one who has gone home. So home is the goal—rarely glimpsed, almost never attained—of all the heroes descended from Odysseus. All literary romance derives from the *Odyssey* and is about rejoining—rejoining a beloved, rejoining parent to child, rejoining a land to its rightful owner or rule. Romance is about putting things aright after some tragedy has put them asunder. It is about restoration of the right relations among things—and going home is where that restoration occurs because that is where it matters most.

In America, the cluster of associations around the word, and its compounds, is perhaps more poignant because of the extraordinary mobility of the American people. From the beginning, we have been a nation constantly moving. As I have suggested elsewhere, the concept of home has a particular resonance for a nation of immigrants, all of whom left one home to seek another; the idea of a "homestead" established a frontier, the new home beyond the home one left in the East; everyone has a "hometown" back there, at least back in time, where stability or at least its image remains alive.

Stability, origins, a sense of oneness, the first clearing in the woods—to go home may be impossible but it is often a driving necessity, or at least a compelling dream. As the heroes of romance beginning with Odysseus know, the route is full of turnings, wanderings, danger. To attempt to go home is to go the long way around, to stray and separate in the hope of finding completeness in reunion, freedom in reintegration with those left behind. In baseball, the journey begins at home, negotiates the twists and turns at first, and often founders far out at the edges of the ordered world at rocky second—the farthest point from home. Whoever remains out there is said to "die" on base. Home is finally beyond reach in a hostile world full of quirks and tricks and hostile folk. There are no dragons in baseball, only shortstops, but they can emerge from nowhere to cut one down.

And when it is given one to round third, a long journey seemingly over, the end in sight, then the hunger for home, the drive to rejoin one's earlier self and one's fellows, is a pressing, growing, screaming in the blood. Often the effort fails, the hunger is unsatisfied as the catcher bars fulfillment, as the umpire-father is too strong in his denial, as the impossibility of going home again is reenacted in what is often baseball's most violent physical confrontation, swift, savage, down in the dirt, nothing availing.

Or if the attempt, long in planning and execution, works, then the reunion and all it means is total—the runner is a returned hero, and the teammates are for an instant all true family. Until the attempt is tried again. A "home run" is the definitive kill, the overcoming of obstacle at one stroke, the gratification instantaneous in knowing one has earned a risk-free journey out, around, and back—a journey to be taken at a leisurely pace (but not too leisurely) so as to savor the freedom, the magical invulnerability, from denial or delay.

Virtually innumerable are the dangers, the faces of failure one can meet if one is fortunate enough even to leave home. Most efforts fail. Failure to achieve the first leg of the voyage is extremely likely. In no game of ours is failure so omnipresent as it is for the batter who would be the runner. The young batter who would light out from home, so as to return bearing fame and the spoils of success, is most often simply out, unable to leave and therefore never to know until the next try whether he or she can ever be more than simply a vessel of desire.

The tale of leaving and seeking home is told in as many ways as one can imagine, and there still occur every season plays on the field that even the most experienced baseball people say they have never seen before. The random events, the variety of incidents, the different ways various personalities react to pressure, the passion poured into the quest to win—all are organized by the rhythms of the innings, by the metric of the count and the pitcher's rhythm, and by the cool geometry that is underfoot and overarching.

Repetition within immutable lines and rules; baseball is counterpoint: stability vying with volatility, tradition with the quest for a new edge, ancient rhythms and ever-new blood—an oft-told tale, repeated in every game in every season, season after season. If this is the tale told, who tells it? Clearly, the players who enact it thereby also tell it. But the other true tellers of the narrative are those for whom it is played. If baseball is a narrative, an epic of exile and return, a vast, communal poem about separation, loss, and the hope for reunion—if baseball is a Romance Epic—it is finally told by the audience. It is the Romance Epic of homecoming America sings to itself.

Where does America sing this poem, say this story? Wherever baseball gathers. Let me tell you of one gathering that will stand for all the others, for while we have considered the abstract principles and patterns of our narrative, and its mythic fable, it is meet to be most concrete when thinking on the tellers of the tale, for in them, too, the narrative lives.

The Marriott Pavilion Hotel in St. Louis is hard by the ballpark. It consists of a pair of towers linked by a vast lobby and corridors and a ramp, the cavernous space interspersed with plants and some chairs and columns, the floor of this cavern covered by a carpeting the color of a fresh bruise. During the National League Championship Series between St. Louis and San Francisco in 1987, the lobby was ablaze—with Cardinal crimson on hats, jackets, sweaters, scarves, ties. Here and there one glimpsed the orange-and-black of the House of Lurie, as a Giant rooter, like some lonely fish, wove its way across a scarlet coral reef, alive and breathing in the cavernous deep. But such creatures were rare.

By mid-morning, the lobby is crowded, and will remain crowded, except during the game, until about 2 A.M., then to fill up by nine and wait the long day until game time. There are the smiling, middle-aged couples, festooned in buttons and insignia, this day yet another convention day in a lifetime of conventioneering; the groups of teenage boys, in the plumage of scarlet windbreakers, like young birds craning their necks for the nourishment of a glimpse; a trio of natty young men, one with a briefcase, who are—I learn later from a hapless friend—pickpockets. They work the elevators, one to hold the door, one to feign having caught his shoe in the crack between floor and car, one to lift the wallet of the first person to assist. By a plant or a coffee shop, always alone, white hair crisply permed, in electric blue or purple pants suit, holding an autograph book, is a grandmotherly woman, smiling distractedly, waiting for a hero. There are always some single men in their forties, in nondescript clothes, hair slightly awry, eyes burning with fatigue and anticipation; they are the religiously obsessed, drawn by a vision in their heads that will not give them peace. They stand apart and wait for hours in this holy place. Very different are the middle-aged teenagers, men in groups, all mid-forties, who shout and drink the day away, some with young women in black leather pants and scarlet T-shirts, their laughter and their manner frenzied. At the back of the lobby, down on a lower level, around a low table, sit this morning the Giants' manager and coaches. They are like chiefs at a gathering of the clan, planning strategy, ignoring the celebrants while absorbing their energy.

Across the lobby of the Marriott Pavilion Hotel march in precision a group of young people, all in their twenties, network technicians off to work. The men are all bearded, in down jackets and jeans, the women in sweaters and beads and leg warmers. All wear some kind of boot. They are the flower children of High Tech. The future is theirs and they know it. They stride, silent and confident, like trainees at McKinsey. The chosen.

The largest contingent, in groups of three or four, is men in middle age and older, in suits and resplendent ties and polished shoes, some with cigars; they have seamed faces and eyes that seem to squint even in shade. They stand with the poised patience born of watching a dozen thousand baseball games—the scouts, the farm directors, the active or former coaches, the minor league general managers, retired ballplayers or umpires, former managers, the sporting goods representatives who once played the outfield. These are the true Baseball people. Among them one spots a younger face, the front office worker with a club, someone in PR or Promotion, some assistant to a general manager. There is an owner here and there, a broadcaster in his plumage, a club financial officer, a Director of Player Development representing his team at the Series. There are corporate sponsors, an occasional agent, someone's glistening lawyer, a television executive. And through it all, recognizable by their rumpled casualness and weary eyes, are the working press, mostly the beat writers and columnists, occasionally a magazine writer—the daily press in mismatched jackets and trousers, shirts open, barely recovered from filing, always looking for the next hook, the next lead, the telling anecdote. Distracted, intense, listening to three conversations and holding forth in two, the journalists circulate according to a pecking order known only to them. When they sit, it is as if there were a cosmic seating chart; no one is ever in the wrong group. Now they move through the crowd as the crowd shifts and eddies and pauses and waits, anticipating the next game, replaying last night's contest, last week's, last year's.

Add the groupies, the sharpies, the hangers-on, the family members, the deal-makers, the ticket hustlers, the fathers who aim and loose their children like heat-seeking missiles to bring down an autograph, the busloads of one-time fans, bewildered and giddy—in short, everyone but the players, who never appear in the lobby until it is all over—and the sound is a high, constant hum, a vast buzz of a million bees, the sound almost palpable and, for hours, never varying in pitch or intensity as anecdote vies with anecdote or joke or gossip or monologue or rude ribbing, so reminiscent of the clubhouse. It is the sound of tip and critique and prediction and second-guessing, of nasty crack and generous assessment, of memory cutting across memory, supplementing and correcting and coloring the tale, all the crosscutting, overlapping, salty, blunt, nostalgic, sweet conversation about only one subject—Baseball.

Here the oft-told tale that is the game is told again. It is told always in the present tense, in a paratactic style that reflects the game's seamless, cumulative character, each event linked to the last and creating the context for the next—a style almost Biblical in its continuity and instinct for typology. It is told in a tone at once elegiac, sharply etched, inclusive of all nuance. Baseball people have the keenest eyes for the telling detail I have ever known. This might be an overheard moment—one erect, white-haired old man to two peers:

"So now Tebbetts is catching in Boston, he tells me last winter, and Parnell is pitching, it's against New York, and it's a brutal day, no wind, hot, rainy, it's going to pour and they want to get the game in, and Joe Gordon splits his thumb going into second when Junior Stevens steps on his hand, he can't pivot, and now it's the eighth, tie score, and Bobby Brown comes up with two out and Bauer sitting on third and Birdie says to Ed Hurley who's got the plate, 'This is the Doctor, Ed, this is a left-handed doctor . . .'" And it goes on, extending itself by loops and symmetrical segments and reiterations just the way the game does, as if it were yesterday and not August 1949.

Such is the talk in the lobby of the Marriott Pavilion Hotel in St. Louis during the League Championship Series in the first week of October 1987, as it was also in lobbies in San Francisco and Detroit and Minneapolis, as it is every time Baseball gathers—whether in clubhouse, bus, or airplane. This is the talk in lobbies across some two thousand games a season, as it has been season after season, since the 1870s, before artificial turf and domes, before air travel, before night baseball—back to the days of trains and rooming houses and front porches, the first versions of the lobby.

So Ned Hanlon must have talked, and McGraw, and Speaker and Miller Huggins and even Connie Mack; so Sisler may have talked and Jackie, surely Durocher and Stengel, and so talk Yogi and Ernie and Whitey and Lasorda and Cashen and Sparky and Willie Mays and all the thousands they entail; the players and coaches and scouts and managers and umpires, somewhere they all talk. But the fullest, most expansive, most public talk is the talk in the lobby, baseball's second-favorite venue. The lobby is the park of talk; it is the enclosed place where the game is truly told, because told again and again. Each time it is played and replayed in the telling, the fable is refined, the nuances burnished the color of old silver. The memories in baseball become sharpest as they recede, for the art of telling improves with age.

Let me close in the tone and style of our national narrative: So now, I'm standing in the lobby of the Marriott in St. Louis in October of '87 and I see this crowd, so happy with itself, all talking baseball, and I want to be in this game, so I spend two hours moving about, listening to them talk the game and hearing them getting it right, working at the fine points the way players in the big leagues do, and it comes to me slowly, around noon, that this, *this*, is what Aristotle must have meant by the imitation of an action.

EPILOGUE

Beginning with the conviction that our use of "free time" told us about ourselves as a people, I posed—more for myself thinking on baseball than to persuade the reader—the question: Is not freedom the fulfillment of the promise of an energetic, complex order? Clearly I believe the answer is yes, and clearly, therefore, I believe we cherish as Americans a game wherein freedom and reunion are both possible. Baseball fulfills the promise America made itself to cherish the individual while recognizing the overarching claims of the group. It sends its players out in order to return again, allowing all the freedom to accomplish great things in a dangerous world. So baseball restates a version of America's promises every time it is played. The playing of the game is a restatement of the promises that we can all be free, that we can all succeed.

So games, contests, sports reiterate the purpose of freedom every time they are enacted—the purpose being to show how to be free and to be complete and connected, unimpeded and integrated, all at once. That is the role of leisure, and if leisure were a god, rather than Aristotle's version of the highest human state, sport would be a constant reminder—not a faded remnant—of that transcendent or sacred being. This is so because sport—no matter how cheapened (and it need not be) or commercialized (and it often is) or distant from an external ideal (which it may never have approached)—contains within itself, as a self-transforming activity, fueled by instinct and intellect alike, the motive for freedom. The very elaborations of a sport—its internal conventions of all kinds, its ceremonies, its endless meshes entangling itself—are for the purpose of training and testing (perhaps by defeating) and rewarding the rousing motion within us to find a moment (or more) of freedom. Freedom is that state where energy and order merge and all complexity is purified into a simple coherence, a fitness of parts and purpose and passions that cannot be surpassed and whose goal could only be to be itself.

If we have known freedom, then we love it; if we love freedom, then we fear, at some level (individually or collectively), its loss. And then we cherish sport. As our forebears did, we remind ourselves through sport of what, here on earth, is our noblest hope. Through sport, we re-create our daily portion of freedom, in public.

AFTERWORD

Marcus Giamatti

There was a period of time, long ago, when my father and I lived in New York City simultaneously. He in a hotel room in Midtown, and I in a dingy apartment on the Upper West Side. Occasionally, the anxious head-chatter of my young-actor-adrift-in-the-big-city routine would be mercifully interrupted by one of my father's late-night phone calls. After a day of work, my father relished the opportunity to relax in his room, a yellow legal pad in hand, and ruminate.

For him, this was a moment of flow. A pause seized to craft ideas and thoughts. Thoughts for this very book you hold in your hands. Our conversation would always start with a discourse on baseball—the connective glue in our lives, from my boyhood to that present moment—including, of course, the current state of our beloved Boston Red

Sox. (Through the fate of lineage, I had inherited this particularly reckless New England disease.) My father's secondary impetus here was to pick my brain about some experiences that were unique to me—those of the athlete. While he was an incredible student of sports—and, above all, baseball (obviously)—he had never ventured as a player beyond his childhood backyard efforts. I had been a student athlete, playing baseball and soccer and swimming through college. I was beyond humbled that my father had a true desire to know my insights, and experiences, for this book. And, subsequently, that he found them useful. After we said goodnight and retreated to our separate corners of that sleeping Goliath, I was always filled with such a keen sense of clarity. Such a keen sense of connection. As to one whose heart is seen and, in turn, sees. The familiar resonated, and in that precious time where it glowed, I took comfort that I was not alone. I had him. And he had me. On our journey's arc, our relationship had evolved to that natural next step—that of maturity. That of a shared reverence. That of friendship.

If I had only known how tragically brief this newfound configuration would be. Blindsided, that unique period was snuffed out before it really began. And this mountain in my life, against a brilliant blaze of light, one beautiful September afternoon just disappeared.

Only a few short days after my father's sudden death, I found myself alone in the kitchen of my mother's house, face-to-face with a freshly opened box of books. Books that only moments before had been delivered to her doorstep. My father never saw the publication of *Take Time for Paradise*. The irony of the title became clear in that instant. Here was a man who worked so hard, rarely took a break, and died so young. Did he ever in his life have a chance to "take the time"? And if so, when? I wonder . . .

Solace comes with a cross-fade montage of memory. For we did have baseball. As a boy, on any given summer Saturday afternoon you might find me upstairs in my room, in full daydream recline, surrounded by the images of my baseball heroes. There I would lie in wait, till I heard my father's gleeful command from somewhere in the depths of our family home. I had champed at the bit since daybreak for this call to arms. A call that signaled the beginning of my father's self-imposed hiatus from the weekend correction of students' papers—from work. It was a call that hustled us up to grab our mitts and Red Sox hats from a broom closet in the kitchen. Now clad for battle, our hearts filled with possibility—the two of us seemingly bound on some sacred mission like Telemachus and Odysseus—we made our purposeful exit through an antiquated tin screen door, out toward the sun. In the oblong, pocked backyard of our house in New Haven, under a blue sky, with a warm June breeze at our backs, we played long toss. Back and forth. No sound but the lone cadence set by the solitary pop of a ball in a mitt. Then a sudden shift, and infield instruction became the mode. My father fired ground balls in my direction with a passion. Always the teacher, he led a supportive tutorial in proper fielder's techniques. Finally came my most beloved slice of the afternoon's adventure: with a flick of his glove, he gave me the familiar signal to assume the position of catcher. Now he, Luis Tiant, and I, Carlton Fisk. A sudden hush fell over the crowd as, with a weathered, buckle shoe, he toed the imaginary rubber, shrugged, and, with a deep sigh, leaned in for the sign, his face calm with focus as he peered down at me over his glasses. With a nod of the head (the selection accepted), he ever so slowly arrived at the set position, checked the runner on first (somewhere over by the garage) . . . and froze. Motionless. I held my breath. Pa's oxford shirt and red chinos billowed in the breeze. The world's clock closed down. And then, with a sudden kick of the leg, an El Tiante twist of the body, and a head jolt thrust heavenward, my father let loose a fastball. Right down the middle. A thunderous clap of leather shook the neighborhood as the ball arrived and nestled tightly in my palm's pocket. Such stillness held as a smile eclipsed his bearded visage. My hero. An instant apprehended. Lassoed. And perfected. Now restored, with a tip of his cap, my father exited the field, back up the porch steps, through that screen door, and returned to work.

Dissolve now, memory, and fade up to nights—school nights at the dinner table, long after mealtime, where I sat, and feigned hard interest in whatever Dickensian novel I had been assigned for class. There among piles of books and manuscripts, against the percussive rhythm of my father's typewriter, I was allowed to accompany him—if the bulk of my homework was completed—and listen to the Red Sox on our Magnavox stereo radio. The voice that narrated this nightly carnival, from faraway exotic lands like Detroit, or Baltimore, was Ned Martin. Like some mystical wizard, Mr. Martin had the power to soothe, elate, or destroy us. He had control over our very baseball existence. I was convinced that my father had a personal, cerebral pipeline set up with him. For only Ned Martin had the power to interrupt my father from the tick-tack of his creation. Only Ned Martin could make my father stop. Stop and sit back, at a crucial point in the game, and close his eyes in meditation.

"Concentrate your forces, boy," my father would say with serene assurance. On cue, I would follow suit, and imitate his every sensibility—anything to help will the outcome of that evening's quest in favor of our most noble team. So there we sat, eyes closed, my father and I, in deep concentration, as the wizard Martin colored the room in shades of suspense, helped us to feel, and then, inevitably, helped us to reason.

On Sundays, we didn't go to church. We went to Fenway Park. Fenway Park, where my grandfather took my father as a boy. Fenway Park, where we headed, predawn, in my father's yellow VW Bug. The intention was to arrive as early as possible, and wander the ballpark's neighborhood for hours, in order to fully absorb the aura of that mythic place. Fenway Park, where the universal language of Baseball was, and is, still spoken. Fenway Park, where, in those days, Dame Mutability roamed the stands come the late innings, and Rice, Lynn, and Evans roamed the outfield. Fenway Park, where, on these magnificent afternoons, out in the bleachers, my father never seemed more relaxed. His arms thrown back. His face arched toward the sun. He was alive. Here, at Fenway, my father was never more animated. His voice, that of a sonic boom, would shake the Old Yard's very foundation as he leaped in the air with joy. Or with protest. His spirit never more radiant as he commiserated with our fellow fans. I still sense his arm around my shoulder, as he indicated, taught, and helped me to appreciate. My father existed wholly in the clarity of that moment. Free. And I followed. Yes, Fenway Park. There in baseball's Garden of Paradise, in memory's glorious snapshot, my father sits peacefully, locked in a timeless place, where the connection to all of "it" intersected. For on these pilgrimages, our common bond solidified around the game and its deeper lessons, applicable to life, which he imparted.

Each season is a quest. Each game a journey. A journey that embodies its own unique, peculiar process. A process whose very foundation is built on the game's elusive principles of simplicity: one pitch at a time, one at bat at a time, and one game at a time. And during this process (a process you must trust and commit to), if you are willing to make the constant, necessary adjustments in order to succeed, to stay in the moment, and to have the conviction of awareness to never carry your last success, or miscue, with you to the plate, and, most important, after the mastery of these details, if you can remain mindful that the voyage *is* the thing—you will be rewarded. And that reward, no matter the journey's outcome—because the outcome is always a mystery—will be the character you acquired, for having persevered.

But whether one has the discipline to make this sport's Zen puzzle second nature or not, my father implored passionate vigil for the very essence of this beautiful game. Its endless possibilities. Its potential for surprise, failure, redemption, and hope. The hope that is baseball. Value for the heart, mind, and soul resides here. Honor it. Respect it. For the game fulfills an essential need. A specific, individual release. A release in cahoots with an opportunity to dream . . . that is sacred. So therefore we made the time. Because it mattered. Because what it gave, and still gives, ultimately, over the years, throughout childhood, and into adulthood, is a precious connection. A connection to something more valuable than even the game can realize in its patterns and rituals. And with each new day, each new game, there comes another chance to reconnect. Reconnect to a simpler time. A late-night phone call; the pop of a ball in a mitt; a stroll around that old New England neighborhood where a Green Monster lurks; a father's hand on his son's shoulder, there under the sun, in an open green space. I cherish such comfort received in this reconnection. This gift. And thus, with the ritual observance, presently still, of each day's baseball game, I ride reconnection's wave, and let it carry me back. Back to our dining room table in New Haven. There, the wizard Martin narrates, and my father types. And we are together again. Heart to heart. We have each other. And with the crack of the bat, the roar of the crowd, for a moment, all is right in the world. And once again, we are not alone.

MARCUS GIAMATTI is the eldest of Bart Giamatti's three children. He is an actor, musician, and writer currently living in Los Angeles with his wife and daughter.

NOTES

1. Michael O'Loughlin, *The Garlands of Repose: The Literary Celebration of Civic and Retired Leisure* (Chicago: University of Chicago Press, 1978), xiii, p. 10.
2. For play as autotelic, and games, contests, and sports as versions of rule-bound play, see Allen Guttman, *From Ritual to Record* (New York: Columbia University Press, 1978), Chapter 1. See also his *A Whole New Ball Game* (Chapel Hill: University of North Carolina Press, 1988), Chapter 1.
3. *Ball Game*, pp. 6–8; also *Ritual*, pp. 16*ff.*
4. *Ritual*, p. 55.
5. *Garlands*, pp. 5–6.
6. *Garlands*, p. 6.
7. Aristotle, *Nichomachean Ethics*, 10.7.1177b, 5–6.
8. Aristotle, *Politics*, 1338a–b.
9. *Politics*, 1333a–b, 7–8; see also 1334a, 2; 1334a, 14–15.
10. See Sebastian de Grazia, *Of Time, Work and Leisure* (New York: Twentieth Century, 1962).
11. *Garlands*, p. 10.

12. *Nichomachean Ethics*, 10.7.1177b, 36.

13. *Ritual*, p. 23.

14. *Garlands*, p. 8.

15. As Guttman shows; see *Ritual*, pp. 50–51.

16. See A. B. Giamatti, *The Earthly Paradise and the Renaissance Epic* (Princeton: Princeton University Press, 1966; reprint, New York: W. W. Norton, 1989), for the history of the word *paradise*.

17. I exempt from this all the conventions held by players—the rules about how a game is played. These include all the rules of skill (what to do) and all the rules of behavior (how to appear when you are doing it).

18. *Caddy* or *caddie* derived from the Scots *caudis* and from the French *cadet*, for porter or errand boy. See *caddy* in *Concise Oxford Dictionary of Etymology*, T. F. Hood, ed. (Oxford: Clarendon Press, 1956).

19. See *fun* in *Concise Oxford Dictionary of Etymology*, T. F. Hood, ed. (Oxford: Clarendon Press, 1956).

20. See Richard Sandomir, "The $50 Billion Sports Industry," *Sports inc.*, November 14, 1988, pp. 14–23. I am grateful to Mr. Sandomir for his conversation on this subject with me as well. All other citations are to p. 14*f.*

21. See Harold Seymour, *Baseball: The Early Years* (New York: Oxford University Press, 1960), Chapter 1, for almost all of the early references to baseball.

BIBLIOGRAPHICAL NOTE

I have profited much from the studies by Allen Guttman: *From Ritual to Record* (New York: Columbia University Press, 1978); *Sports Spectators* (New York: Columbia University Press, 1986); and *A Whole New Ball Game* (Chapel Hill: University of North Carolina Press, 1988). All these contain bibliographic guidance on specific sports as well as interpretive essays on sport.

The best book I know on the concept of leisure is the magisterial study by Michael O'Loughlin, *The Garlands of Repose: The Literary Celebration of Civic and Retired Leisure* (Chicago: University of Chicago Press, 1978). Further essential bibliography is given on pp. 289–290, *n.* 5, and p. 291, *n.* 15. I have also found valuable Sebastian de Grazia, *Of Time, Work and Leisure* (New York: Twentieth Century, 1962). For a related thème, that of paradise, see A. B.

Giamatti, *The Earthly Paradise and the Renaissance Epic* (Princeton: Princeton University Press, 1966; reprint, New York: W. W. Norton, 1989).

Aristotle's *Politics* and *Nichomachean Ethics* are cited in the translations in the Loeb Library editions (Harvard University Press). Milton is cited from *The Complete Poetry and Selected Prose of John Milton*, Merritt Hughes, ed. (New York: Macmillan, 1957); Henry Vaughan from *Henry Vaughan: The Complete Poems*, Alan Rudrum, ed. (New Haven: Yale University Press, 1981); Marianne Moore from *The Complete Poems* (New York: Viking-Penguin, 1967, 1981). I learned most of my early baseball history from Harold Seymour, *Baseball: The Early Years* (New York: Oxford University Press, 1960). I owe the reference to Jane Austen to Charles Bronfman of Montreal.

A NOTE ON THE AUTHOR

A. Bartlett Giamatti served as commissioner of Major League Baseball from April 1, 1989, until his death on September 1, 1989. He had previously been the president of the National League, starting in 1986. He was a scholar of the English Renaissance at Yale University, a beloved professor, and later, the university's youngest president.